Daily Devotional Nuggets *for* Women *on the* Go

Frances W. Cox

Kingdom Builders Publications LLC

Daily Devotional Nuggets for Women on the Go
Copyright © 2020 Frances W. Cox
Kingdom Builders Publications

All rights reserved. No part of this book may be reproduced or transmitted in any form or by any means without written permission from the author.

The Scriptural text has been granted permission to Frances W. Cox by www.biblehub.com
The twelve (12) Bible references are noted on Bible Reference page.

ISBN: 978-0-578-79574-4
Library of Congress Control Number:

Printed in the USA

Authored by
Frances W. Cox

Editor
Dr. Lakisha S. Forrester
Kingdom Builders Publications

Cover Design
Frances W. Cox

Picture for Cover
From the personal library of Frances W. Cox

Pictures of Flowers
www.petalrepublic.com

The Pink Dahlia Symbolizes:
femininity, kindness, grace, and everything that is good

PREFACE

This book was written by the author and the Holy Spirit to empower and encourage women through biblical verses that God is with them as they encounter obstacles, roadblocks, indecisions, and impending dangers. The author wants women to know that the same courage and strength God gave many of the people used in the verses can be theirs by committing themselves totally to His precepts.

The terms sister and daughter reflect the personal relationship the author enjoys with the Godhead and how they freely welcome her into the spirit realm. The warmth and intimacy of each response is in accordance with the name of the flower at the beginning of each month that symbolizes the nature and human character of the women who read the verses. The colors of the blooms signify life, health, strength, intellect, healing, love, inner strength, elegance, boldness, and many more human attributes.

Finally, the author asks women to have faith and believe that the same words spoken over two thousand years ago are still speaking to them today. The same spirit of wisdom that instructed Queen Esther to go before the king of Persia to petition the lives of her people and boldly say, "If I perish, then I perish; I am going to see the king" is still well and alive now (4:16). The same Godhead that worked in the hearts and minds of women yesterday still works today.

The Purple Dahlia Symbolizes:
royalty, dignity, and strength

A WORD OF INTIMACY

The king rejoices in your strength, Lord. How great is his joy in the victories you give! You have granted him his heart's desire and have not withheld the request of his lips. Psalm 21:1-2, NIV

Sister, come quickly. King David has left us a Wisdom Nugget. He had a special covering and protection from God. That is why God gave him victories over his enemies and granted him all his requests, except those that went against His precepts. Because we are His daughters and He is our Father, if we want this gift and to receive this special favor too, we must promise to keep His precepts.

Sister, let us reason together. We pray to God, who is our Father, in the name of His Son, in the presence of the Holy Spirit. Therefore, we can call Him 'Daddy,' and call His Son, our Savior, our Intercessor, and our Brother. Because we are now one with Him, His Son, and the Holy Spirit, we live in them and they live in us. We can speak healing over our bodies, and it will happen. All things are possible because we know them, and they know our names.

Sister, let us rejoice as David rejoiced, who said, "I will bless the LORD at all times; His praise *shall* continually *be* in my mouth" (Psalm 34:1, NKJV).

The Blue Dahlia Symbolizes:
new beginnings and a new life

TABLE OF CONTENTS

Preface iii
A Word of Intimacy 4
January 6
February 37
March 66
April 97
May 127
June 158
July 188
August 219
September 250
October 280
November 311
December 341
Scriptures on Faith 373
Scriptures on Prayer 375
Scriptures on Healing 377
Acknowledgments 381
About the Author 382

JANUARY

The Camellia Flower Symbolizes:
love, passion, desire, a longing for someone, and admiration

January 1

This month shall be for you the beginning of months. It shall be the first month of the year for you. Exodus 12:2, ESV

Daughter, you are starting a new beginning. You must leave behind those things that caused grief and pain. Those old burdens and yokes that you carried last year will only weigh you down. You cannot bring them into the new year and receive the blessings I have prepared for you. I have cast them in a sea of forgetfulness. I have cleared the way and created paths for you. I have made plans for you that no one can erase. So greet this day with your head held high. You are the daughter of a King, and I am rich in houses and land.

January 2

Fear not, for I am with you; be not dismayed, for I am your God; I will strengthen you, I will help you, I will uphold you with my righteous right hand. Isaiah 41:10, ESV

I am your Lord and your Keeper. I will hold you up when you are restless. I am your help. So go joyfully into this day. I will guide and protect you from all evil and from those who wish to harm you. You are my daughter which commands my care, love, and protection.

January 3

God is in the midst of her; she shall not be moved; God will help her when morning dawns. Psalm 46:5, ESV

Here I am, precious daughter. Trust me, I have not forsaken you. Look deep within your heart and you shall find me. Can you feel my touch, my breath blowing across your face, and my arms holding you during this stressful time? I am your protector and the lover of your soul. I am in the midst of you wherever you go and whoever you are with. I am here to wake you up and to lay you down at night. I will never leave or forsake you. So dance daughter – dance. Throw your head back and dance. Dance free from all cares and worries. Dance with joy in your heart. Morning is coming and I will be in the midst dancing along with you.

January 4

And my God will supply every need of yours according to his riches in glory in Christ Jesus. Philippians 4:19, ESV

Are you hungry, need clothes, or need a place to live? Are you looking for someone to truly love you for yourself and not what you can do for them? Could it be someone on your job placing stumbling blocks in your path? Whatever it is, here I am, daughter, to fix it for you. Ask me. I have been here all the time, waiting for you to hear me. You have the right to call me 'Daddy' because that is who I AM to you. So greet this day with joy and happiness in your heart. Anything you ask in the name of your Brother, Jesus Christ, Daddy will supply it for you. I am your healer, your provider, and your supplier. I am all you need.

January 5

Do you not know that your bodies are temples of the Holy Spirit, who is in you, whom you have received from God? You are not your own; you were bought at a price. Therefore honor God with your bodies.
1 Corinthians 6:19-20, NIV

Sister, when we become a daughter of our Father, there are some things we cannot do to our bodies because the Holy Spirit lives in it. We cannot fill our bodies with alcohol, drugs, or perform immoral acts and willfully destroy any parts of it. Our bodies are like a church and the church lives in us. We worship and praise God in the natural church. Therefore, we should worship and praise God in the church in us. The Holy Spirit tells us what to say as we pray, praise, and worship our Father. We do not own this church that is in our bodies. God owns it because He created us and purchased us from eternal death with the blood of His Son. So rejoice that you are saved, and greet this day by praising God for salvation and the gift of life.

January 6

Do not be anxious about anything, but in everything by prayer and supplication with thanksgiving let your requests be made known to God. Philippians 4:6, ESV

Daughter, do not let worry overcome you. If you are expecting good or bad news, wondering about it will not bring it any closer to you. If you desire anything, talk to me about it. I already know the answers, but I need to hear you tell me about everything. I am happy when I can hear you call on me, and as daughters always do --thank their fathers for their gifts. So greet this day with a satisfied mind. Your sincere prayers will be answered. I will never forsake you. I will not leave you to face your troubles alone.

January 7

Finally, be strong in the Lord and in the strength of his might. Put on the whole armor of God, that you may be able to stand against the schemes of the devil. Ephesians 6:10-11, ESV

Sister, it is time for you to get radical with your enemies and stop treating them like they are your friends. They have taken your kindness for weakness. You have withstood false accusations and dodged stumbling blocks they have thrown in your path. Be strong and put on God's armor. You were created to be a strong warrior and a daughter of a King. So get ready to face your foes. You will be able to stand against them because your Father will fight the battle for you.

January 8

Can a woman forget her nursing child, that she should have no compassion on the son of her womb? Even these may forget, yet I will not forget you. Isaiah 49:15, ESV

Daughter, I have carried you all these years through grief, pain, and disappointments. How can you even think that I will forget you now? You are a part of me, and I am a part of you. We are two of the same. I am a fixed structure in your life. I will remain here as long as you do not walk away from me. Some may forsake the sons and daughters they brought into this world, but you were created in my image. I will not forsake you or leave you alone. Your thoughts can be my thoughts and your heart can beat to the rhythm of my voice. I know your moves and your ways. I know your likes and the things you disagree with. So greet this day knowing that I am with you and will not leave you defenseless. Believe in me and nothing, I mean nothing will separate you from my love.

January 9

The L̶ord repay you for what you have done, and a full reward be given you by the L̶ord, the God of Israel, under whose wings you have come to take refuge! Ruth 2:12, ESV

Daughter, why are you wasting precious time looking for recognition from man about the work you have performed? Do you not know that I am your supplier and provider? No matter what man may say, your life, as well as his life, are in my hands. When he does wrong by you with your wages, he wrongs me as well and will have to answer to me. I will chastise him, and you shall live to see it. Let not your heart be troubled; I am here to defend you. So go joyfully into this day. You are under my wings. I will protect and repay you openly for your service.

January 10

Be merciful to me, O God, be merciful to me, for in you my soul takes refuge; in the shadow of your wings I will take refuge, till the storms of destruction pass by. Psalm 57:1, ESV

Come quickly, my child. Come and hide in the safety of my wings. I will cover you in the warmth of my feathers. I have often told you that I was the lover of your soul and you can find rest for your weariness and from those who seek to harm you. Under my wings you will find peace, comfort, and security. You will find true love that is safe, pure, and unconditional. So greet this day with a smile on your face. The rest you long for will carry you through this day.

January 11

I will fall upon them like a bear robbed of her cubs; I will tear open their breast, and there I will devour them like a lion, as a wild beast would rip them open. **Hosea 13:8, ESV**

Stop running from your enemies, child. I am here to protect you. You will never need to run as long as you are in my care. You are like a baby to me, and I will fight anything that tries to harm you. All mothers who truly love their children have animal instincts and will tear down any barrier in order to save their children. So be calm and of a good cheer; I will allow no one to hurt a hair on your head or cause you to lose a moment's rest. So walk into today with the joy of safety in your steps. I am watching over you.

January 12

And whatever you ask in prayer, you will receive, if you have faith.
Matthew 21:22, ESV

Sister, if your faith is weak and you need a stronger faith, then ask our Father who is the Author and Finisher of our faith. He can take our faith which may be the size of a mustard seed and grow it so large like a tree where birds and other animals may roost and build their homes in its limbs and branches. That is how He will grow your faith. You do not have to do anything but have a desire to believe that He can and will do that. When you pray, you can ask Him anything and expect to receive it. That is the kind of Father we have. We can go to Him with any problem we may think is small and He will fix it for us. So stop thinking that no one cares. Our Father knows our every need and wants to supply them. He truly cares for you.

January 13

Anyone who does not love does not know God, because God is love.
1 John 4:8, ESV

Come to me, daughter. Your heart is aching and you feel like you do not want to live anymore. There is no reason for you to think that no one cares, because I care. I want to heal your pain and seal your broken heart. I know you thought that person loved you as much as you loved them, but they took advantage of you and trampled on your love. I am the lover of your soul and can heal the cracks and bruises in your heart. Come, let me teach you about love. You see, dear, love is patient and kind. Love is gentle and knows no hatred or jealously. If that person knew me, they would know how to love you because I am love. So rise, shine, and another love will come who knows me and will treat you like the daughter of a King.

January 14

And above all these put on love, which binds everything together in perfect harmony. Colossians 3:14, ESV

Sister, where is your coat of love? Our Father taught us not to hate those who show hatred toward us for the way we are. They cannot embrace the light in us because they do not know the 'Light of the World' as you do. When they show hatred, show them the love of our Father which surpasses all understanding. When you put on your coat of love, nothing harmful can pass through it because it is your covering. There is an aura that surrounds you and takes the negative talk and binds it together just like a medley of peace, love, and happiness. So go forth today, wrapped in the love of our Father. Nothing harmful will come near you.

January 15

*Some trust in chariots and some in horses, but we trust in the name of the L*ORD *our God. Psalm 20:7, ESV*

Sister, listen to this Truth Nugget. Do not put your trust in man nor the instruments they design, because they are only temporal and last for just a short time. That is why you are so disturbed and confused about the decisions you must make. Man can only offer you broken promises and give you trinkets that rust and disappear with time. Our Father has silver and gold. He has gems that sparkle in the sun and give off light in the dark. Put your trust in Him only, and He will not disappoint you. So greet this morning with joy and exaltation. Our God is ahead of you clearing your path and making your way straight.

January 16

Owe no one anything, except to love each other, for the one who loves another has fulfilled the law. Romans 13:8, ESV

Sister, stop allowing yourself to be part of a relationship where you must be obligated to someone. When you are obligated to others, they expect something back from you in return. That obligation can place you at a point where you are stressed out and have to return the same amount in service or finance. Do not feel that you must give everybody money, friendship, or tangible objects just to be with them. You are a daughter of a King and owe no one anything, except to show and give everyone you meet and greet an equal amount of the same love our Father has taught us to give to all. Once you have done that, then you will have fulfilled His law and statutes. So go forth loving, showing, and giving everyone you meet the same agape love our Father gives to us.

January 17

Oh give thanks to the L̲o̲r̲d̲; call upon his name; make known his deeds among the peoples! Psalm 105:1, ESV

Father, you have been my help when I did not know you or myself. You were there for me when I was out there in the world taking it by storm. You lifted me out of the pit of despair and placed my feet on solid ground. You carried me from a valley of insecurity to a tower of strength and courage. You are my great I AM and my strong deliverer. Father, thank you for lifting me up and giving me the desire to believe in myself. I have found healing, peace, and comfort in you; therefore, I shall forever call upon your powerful and holy name. I have witnessed to others of your goodness, your grace, and your faithfulness. You are my strong defense.

January 18

Being confident of this very thing, that He who has begun a good work in you will complete it until the day of Jesus Christ.
Philippians 1:6, NKJV

Daughter, I created you in my image and gave you life. You took that life and modeled it into a beautiful soul. The work I began in you is special and it has drawn several people to live by my precepts. You are admired by many for your modesty and tenacity. Younger women emulate you and want to follow in your footsteps. Older women follow you because they see the wisdom and stable growth in your character. Your life is sustained and will continue to serve as a shining light upon a hill. Go into this day with goodness and mercy following you all the days of your life. You are my jewel, a diamond that came out of the rough that's tough and sparkles from afar.

January 19

Rejoice in hope, be patient in tribulation, be constant in prayer.
Romans 12:12, ESV

Sister, here is another Truth Nugget to live by. Never lose your hope in a moment of despair. Do not be in a hurry. Be patient when you are going through trials in your life. Never lose sight of prayer. This nugget will get you through any problem or struggle that confronts you. Prayer is powerful because it knows no boundaries that can keep it out. So when life throws you a sack of dirt, spread it out, plant some seeds, pray, and watch them grow. If you can remember to do these things when you are down, going through, or just plain out of sorts, heaven will be your home.

January 20

Be still before the LORD and wait patiently for him; fret not yourself over the one who prospers in his way, over the man who carries out evil devices! Psalm 37:7, ESV

Yes, daughter, I know the promotion your colleague received was not right. They know that you should have received the promotion, and in due time you will. I see all things and will reward those who wait patiently for me to intervene. Do not allow this moment to shatter or diminish your hopes and dreams. Do not try to avenge yourself. Your timing and my timing may not be the same, but I will vindicate you. Let peace have its perfect will. When they think not, I will turn the tables over in your behalf. So fret not yourself because of the evil they do. Right will triumph over wrong, and you shall live to see it. Rejoice as you enter this day. Your Father is still in control.

January 21

For he will hide me in his shelter in the day of trouble; he will conceal me under the cover of his tent; he will lift me high upon a rock.
Psalm 27:5, ESV

Fear not, my timid daughter. I have always kept you in my view. I have hidden you under the covering of my tent; no danger can enter this place. I know you cannot see it, but you must trust what I say. Great accomplishments and fortunes await you in the future. You have been chosen to be a leader. Your life will touch so many people and bring about lasting changes in their lives. You will live as I bring these things to pass. Go and greet this day with gladness and joy in your walk. I will preserve you for a new day to come. You shall be lifted high where men may see your good works and will glorify me, your Father in heaven.

January 22

For by grace you have been saved through faith. And this is not your own doing; it is the gift of God. Ephesians 2:8, ESV

Sister, here is a Wisdom Nugget for you. "Now faith is the substance of things hoped for, the evidence of things not seen" (Hebrews 11:1, KJV). We often confuse faith with belief, but the two are not the same. Anyone can believe in something, even a person who does not love our Father has a belief. But the difference is that our faith is given to us as a gift from our Father. This faith is a result of grace given through the sacrificial death of Jesus, our Savior, and our Brother. You have an unshakeable faith that has been with you since your youth. You have been strong to overcome obstacles placed in your way. Your faith will carry you to higher heights.

January 23

Let not steadfast love and faithfulness forsake you; bind them around your neck; write them on the tablet of your heart. So you will find favor and good success in the sight of God and man. Proverbs 3:3-4, ESV

Sister, let me tell you how to find favor in the eyes of our Father and the people you see every day. Show love to all you meet and do not forget to be kind and loyal to those in your care or service. This nugget will carry you a long way. So start today by placing it in your heart and you will see blessings and success shower you like raindrops in the spring.

January 24

And we know that for those who love God all things work together for good, for those who are called according to his purpose.
Romans 8:28, ESV

Daughter, do not focus on your injuries, your afflictions, or your health. Leave that to me. Focus on me and the love I have for you. Concentrate on the time when you will be free of your pain and sorrow. There must be some sad days as well as happy days. You were called for my purpose and for such a time as this. There is much work for you to do. Start preparing yourself now. You will need all your mental capabilities to be at work. These things have happened in your body to be a testimonial to others that they can do all things because I will give them strength to overcome all barriers that will rise up against them. So be strong and resist the enemy who will try and distract you. Go into this day with a leap in your heart. I am here to lift and carry you wherever you must go.

January 25

My little children, I am writing these things to you so that you may not sin. But if anyone does sin, we have an advocate with the Father, Jesus Christ the righteous. 1 John 2:1, ESV

Sister, here is another Wisdom Nugget. Stop beating up yourself when you commit wrong and know it is wrong. You can go before your Father who can see well beyond your errors and see your future. He is your Father and you are His daughter. It saddens Him when we do not understand His caring heart. He is quick to forgive because our Brother is standing between heaven and hell as our intercessor, speaking to our Him on our behalf. So leap into this day with joy and gladness that you have an advocator who will carry your wrongs before our Father. And because He is righteous, you will be told to go and not do the same things again.

January 26

Strive for peace with everyone, and for the holiness without which no one will see the Lord. Hebrews 12:14, ESV

Sister, here is a third Truth Nugget. We must have peace with one another if we want to see our Father and our loved ones when we leave this earth. It is written that unless we are holy, which is God-like in our ways and talk, we will never see our Father. Therefore, devote your time to showing peace and engaging in peaceful activities rather than division. Associate with people abiding in the same peaceful beliefs as you and you will be on the right path. Avoid gatherings that condemn, judge, and violate the rights of others. So enter this day with hope, faith, and love in your heart and peace will enter your life.

January 27

Until now you have asked nothing in my name. Ask, and you will receive, that your joy may be full. John 16:24, ESV

My precious child, you can come to me at any time and tell me what is on your mind. You never have to wait because I am always here. I know your needs because that is what a father does. It is his duty to know the needs of his children. You have been an obedient child. You have kept my commandments, even when you were tempted by your friends and went the wrong way. It was during those times that I heard less of you. But you always found your way back home. Daughter, you can call me anytime and I will answer. My ear is not too heavy that I will not recognize your voice. Whatever your heart desires, you may ask me, and I will supply all your needs. It is my duty as your Father to provide joy and happiness in knowing me. So arise and face this day joyfully. Wherever you go, joy and happiness will follow you.

January 28

Let your speech always be gracious, seasoned with salt, so that you may know how you ought to answer each person.
Colossians 4:6, ESV

Sister, stop being so harsh and brazen as you talk to others. You may not know who you are talking to. Some may be angels in disguise that our Father has sent before you to help you on your way to success. Always season your conversations with a dash of kindness and a pinch of love and respect. A little seasoning goes a long way in gaining lasting friends and it will give you an advantage in letting you know how to answer questions that are presented to you. A little seasoning is a steppingstone to your future. So as you walk into tomorrow, carry a pinch of season with you to give flavor to your conversations.

January 29

And rend your hearts and not your garments. Return to the LORD your God, for he is gracious and merciful, slow to anger, and abounding in steadfast love; and he relents over disaster. Joel 2:13, ESV

Daughter, my heart is sad because you have left me without a word of concern. It is not the clothes that have caused you to depart from my ways because they have no heart or soul. You must look within your heart and remove those thoughts that separate us. I will not hold this act against you. Go into this day filled with my love; I will guide you always.

January 30

Beloved, if God so loved us, we also ought to love one another.
1 John 4:11, ESV

Daughter, you must teach and show others how to love as I have loved you. As I gave my Son's life for you, John 15:13 teaches you that the greatest love that you can show is to also give your life for others. So run into this day with the love of all people on your lips.

January 31

__Love does no wrong to a neighbor; therefore love is the fulfilling of the law. Romans 13:10, ESV__

Sister, this Love Nugget is based on the Law of Moses and comes from the last five laws of the Ten Commandments in the Old Testament. According to the Apostle Paul, if we are to keep these laws, we must deal with our neighbors justly. We must learn to love them as we love ourselves (Matthew 22:39), and treat them as we would like to be treated. In doing so, we fulfill the law. So greet this day by loving your neighbor. Your Father rewards those who are obedient.

FEBRUARY

The Ballerina Tulip Symbolizes:
love, opportunity, advancement, and aspiration.

February 1

But the LORD said to Samuel, "Do not look on his appearance or on the height of his stature, because I have rejected him. For the LORD sees not as man sees: man looks on the outward appearance, but the LORD looks on the heart." 1 Samuel 16:7, ESV

Sister, stop focusing on positions and titles. These are material things and they will not last long. Furthermore, our Father has placed a limit on these things. Focus on what our Father has given you. Focus on those things that are fulfilling and lasting in Him. He has given you a sound body, a pure heart, and an understanding mind. These are the attributes that will help you to conquer and reach your goals. Go forth with inward beauty. Your Father will magnify it.

February 2

But they who wait for the LORD shall renew their strength; they shall mount up with wings like eagles; they shall run and not be weary; they shall walk and not faint. Isaiah 40:31, ESV

Sister, do not be in such a hurry to climb the ladder of success. Wait until you hear from our Father who can see your future. He will give you strength to face your difficulties. Why take this journey alone when you can run and walk with our Father? He will carry you if you faint. So get up and face this day with joy. Our Father will go with you on this journey.

February 3

For whatever was written in former days was written for our instruction, that through endurance and through the encouragement of the Scriptures we might have hope. Romans 15:4, ESV

Sister, our Father wants us to know that those verses we read in the Scriptures were written for us so that when we face similar trials in our own lives, we will know how to overcome them. They are written to show us that if these people conquered their problems and had the strength to endure in spite of odds against them, we too, can endure. These verses will give us hope and will encourage us when we feel like giving up. So rise up, sister. There is hope for your future.

February 4

The LORD your God is in your midst, a mighty one who will save; he will rejoice over you with gladness; he will quiet you by his love; he will exult over you with loud singing. Zephaniah 3:17, ESV

Look no further, dear. Here I am. I have been right here in your midst all the time. I have watched you laugh, and my heart was saddened when you cried. I am always here to comfort you when you are alone and when your heart is broken. My love for you is always fresh and will surround you with gladness and joy. I will lift you up out of your valleys of despair, wrap you in my arms, and love you as a father should love his princess. So skip into this day with me watching and guiding your every step. I will never take my eyes off you or leave you alone.

February 5

So Sarah laughed to herself, saying, "After I am worn out, and my lord is old, shall I have pleasure?" Genesis 18:12, ESV

Never doubt my words, daughter. Happiness and bliss can be yours even at your age. All things are possible for anyone who believes in miracles. Remember, Sarah was ninety years of age when she had Isaac. If I can cause her to have pleasure and a son at her age, will I not do the same for you? I am your Father and because you are my daughter, all things are possible if you just believe. Go forth into this day with joy and believe that you will have those things you only dream about. You are as young as you wish to be in your mind. I am faithful to those who are my followers. Even the father of your children knows my faithfulness; he has tried me and found that my words never come back empty or void.

February 6

May the God of hope fill you with all joy and peace in believing, so that by the power of the Holy Spirit you may abound in hope.
Romans 15:13, ESV

Daughter, I have filled you with the gifts of the Holy Spirit so that you may have hope instead of fear and despair. You will have joy when you go through struggles, trials, and oppositions. Love will follow you wherever you walk. It will lead you into paths of righteousness and will cover you when you stand before those in authority. There is peace within you to calm you when anxiety, pain, and trouble enter your heart. Faith will help you to call things that are not seen into things that are seen. Hope will be your gateway to greatness. Without hope, all things good are lost. I will never leave you hopeless or alone.

February 7

You are altogether beautiful, my love; there is no flaw in you.
Song of Solomon 4:7, ESV

Your beauty is deeper than your outer appearance, child. It is on the inside and it radiates outward like a shining star. You are one of my beautiful creations. Your glow is so powerful that it captures the very essence of peace. People are drawn into your beauty and want to be a part of it. Your appearance invites joy, comfort, and happiness. You are an example of my handiwork and you model it very well. Enter into this day with goodness and peace showering you as you meet those who know no peace. Your beauty will captivate their hearts and turn their sadness into happiness. You are an ambassador of my love, peace, and joy. So walk proudly with dignity and honor.

February 8

Charm is deceitful, and beauty is vain, but a woman who fears the LORD is to be praised. Proverbs 31:30, ESV

Sister, there are some women who are impressed with enticing others with their charm and beauty. It is cunning and arrogant for us to behave in such manners. Our Father did not create us to allure men for our comfort. He formed us to be a beacon to show the world the beauty of living for Christ. Our Father's desire is that we will not be ashamed of our inward beauty but to show others grace. When we fear our Father for his majesty, greatness, and righteous judgment, He and the world will praise us for truth and our integrity. So go forth with inward beauty that will change the hearts and minds of women bound with deceit and vanity.

February 9

Let no corrupting talk come out of your mouths, but only such as is good for building up, as fits the occasion, that it may give grace to those who hear. Ephesians 4:29, ESV

Sister, come quick. Here is a Grace Nugget our Father wants us to give to His followers. It is fitting that we do not become double-tongued, talking to believers and nonbelievers about the love of our Father in public, but tearing them down when we are alone. Our mission is to build up the Body of Christ by encouraging others to work for the kingdom of God so they may have grace and mercy at the close of the day when He calls them home. So go forth showing the mercy and grace of our Father. He is a jealous God, but slow to anger. He does not like for us to place any god before Him.

February 10

And after you have suffered a little while, the God of all grace, who has called you to his eternal glory in Christ, will himself restore, confirm, strengthen, and establish you. 1 Peter 5:10, ESV

Daughter, I feel your pain and misery. I am aware of your suffering. I am hurting too, because I saw the disobedience shown toward me when you broke your promise to me. You must endure until my grace flourishes within you and make you whole again. You are going through a time in which you are blaming yourself. There is unrest in your heart. My grace will not enter where there is no peace. Calm yourself by resting in my love. I have not left you alone to bear this burden. I am ready to restore your strength, confidence, and place in the kingdom of daughters who desire to honor and obey my statutes. Go gladly into this day telling others of the love and grace that I offer.

February 11

All glorious is the princess in her chamber, with robes interwoven with gold. Psalm 45:13, ESV

Men of the earth, stand aside and make way for my daughter. I have prepared and dressed her in grace, love, and joy. Her robe is trimmed in refined gold that covers her head down to her feet. She walks in beauty and her steps are ordered according to my precepts. She smells like the blossoms from the Lily of the Valley and the petals from the Rose of Sharon. She is filled with special gifts that show that she is a branch growing from the True Vine which is Jesus Christ. She does not know the evil ways of the world or strive to be a part of it. Honor and respect her for what she represents and who she is. So, daughter, go into this day walking and talking as the princess that you were taught to be. I will supply all your needs according to my riches in glory.

February 12

In the same way, let your light shine before others, so that they may see your good works and give glory to your Father who is in heaven.
Matthew 5:16, ESV

Sister, you need to stop hiding your gifts. Our Father is not pleased with that. He has created you as a shining light to go before His people to share His word with them. When you hide His words, the enemy is happy. His main goal is to enter the hearts and minds of believers and try to sway them away from our Father. You must stand your ground, be strong in our Father's words, and go take the position that He has given you. We have a duty to carry out on the battlefield of life so others may see our good works and glorify our Father in heaven. Let your light shine so our Father may see it from His throne in heaven. So run into this day with gladness in your feet.

February 13

Show yourself in all respects to be a model of good works, and in your teaching show integrity, dignity, and sound speech that cannot be condemned, so that an opponent may be put to shame, having nothing evil to say about us. Titus 2:7-8, ESV

Sister, come and hear this Integrity Nugget we must observe. As we go about our daily work, we must model ourselves as women chosen by our Father to carry His truth. Being chosen does not mean we have to preach or teach from a pulpit or podium. But it does mean that because we know Him and He knows us, we are also His disciples and must follow Him. We should speak truth in a way that those who hear us will not dare question the validity of our report. When we speak truth with integrity this day, it will bring us peace and joy.

February 14

Let no one despise you for your youth, but set the believers an example in speech, in conduct, in love, in faith, in purity. 1 Timothy 4:12, ESV

Here is another Wisdom Nugget, sister. Whether you are old or young, let no one intimidate you by questioning the authority in which you speak truth. Your truth comes from our Father and the Holy Spirit who live within you. Let them be put to shame for trying to suppress you because of your age. Conduct yourself in such a way that they will be amazed and astonished at the words of wisdom that fall from your lips. So go into this day with confidence that whatever you say, your Father has already approved and sealed it.

February 15

Do not be conformed to this world, but be transformed by the renewal of your mind, that by testing you may discern what is the will of God, what is good and acceptable and perfect. Romans 12:2, ESV

Sister, you cannot be a part of this world or even try to change yourself to fit in it. You were chosen as a daughter to be in the world but not of the world. No one can continue to be hot or cold at the same time while speaking the words of our Father. It is like a two-headed animal. He will spew them out of His mouth because this is a lukewarm person. Your mission is to change the hearts and minds of people back to our Father by offering them eternal life through Jesus Christ. Because you are stronger and persistent in your ways, they were not meant to change you. You know your Father's precepts. He taught them to you so you would not forget them. So greet this day with wisdom and understanding. Your Father will give you discernment to know His will and to do His will.

February 16

The one who rejects me and does not receive my words has a judge; the word that I have spoken will judge him on the last day.
John 12:48, ESV

Listen to this Judgment Nugget, sister. Our Father says that anyone who refuses to hear our words and turn from Him to serve other gods will be judged in the final day. The same words they disregard will be used against them in the judgment. We must be careful to speak truth and honesty as we tell others about our Father and the love and mercy that He has available to them. Let us go into this day with a willing mind to fill the ears of those who will listen so they will not be lost on their final day of earth.

February 17

Whatever you do, work heartily, as for the Lord and not for men, knowing that from the Lord you will receive the inheritance as your reward. You are serving the Lord Christ. Colossians 3:23-24, ESV

Come, here is another Inheritance Nugget. Sister, we must work as if it is our last day to receive this nugget. This is one we really need to put in our box of blessings from our Father. There is one important thing we must remember: The work we do is not earthly work, but it is kingdom building work. This kind of work is not done to receive money. It is building the kingdom of God by bringing souls to His altar of grace. Our Father will reward us if we remain faithful in serving His Son, Jesus Christ. So, sister, we will enter this day prepared to work in our Father's kingdom. When we work for the kingdom, we are also working for the future and for the lives of our children. This is the legacy and inheritance we will leave for them.

February 18

For God will bring every deed into judgment, with every secret thing, whether good or evil. Ecclesiastes 12:14, ESV

Sister, never think that you can hide anything from our Father; He sees all and knows all. It is better to bring anything done in secret before Him and allow Him to pass judgment on you. Trying to hide it from Him will only cause you more hurt and pain. So release the thing that is hidden. To hold onto it in your heart and mind will only bring damnation to your soul in the day of judgment. Our Father is faithful to forgive and will cast the hidden deed in a sea of forgetfulness, never to bring it up again. So greet this day with a renewed mind and soul. Rejoice and be exceedingly glad, for great is your reward in heaven.

February 19

Then he dreamed another dream and told it to his brothers and said, "Behold, I have dreamed another dream. Behold, the sun, the moon, and eleven stars were bowing down to me." Genesis 37:9, ESV

Sister, do not throw your dreams away. It may take a long time, but keep trusting our Father and they will come to pass. Remember, Joseph's brothers called him the dreamer. He dreamed that the sun, moon, and eleven stars bowed down to him. His father rebuked him and said that he, his mother, and eleven brothers would never bow to him. His brothers were jealous and plotted to kill him. They sold him to a caravan of Midianites on their way to Egypt. Well, after twenty years, they all bowed down to him in Egypt where he was second in charge to the king. So you see, your dreams may take years, but our father is faithful. No matter how long it takes, he never forgets His promises. Never give up on your dreams; and most importantly, never give up on our Father.

February 20

No temptation has overtaken you that is not common to man. God is faithful, and he will not let you be tempted beyond your ability, but with the temptation he will also provide the way of escape, that you may be able to endure it. 1 Corinthians 10:13, ESV

Sister, come and listen to this Endurance Nugget. There is no earthly desire or entanglement that our Father is not aware of; He will not allow it to overcome you. He knows your comings and your goings as well as when you lay down and when you get up. Nothing escapes His eyes and ears. He will give you the willpower to endure temptation, no matter what it is. He will also provide a way of escape that will not cause grief or harm to your body. Our Father is faithful and will do exactly what He says He will do. So arise and greet this day with confidence that no matter what comes your way, you will have the endurance to survive. He will give you the added faith and the added strength to overcome your difficulties.

February 21

It is better to take refuge in the LORD than to trust in man.
Psalm 118:8, ESV

Sister, when you are tired, weary, and there is no place to go, you can always find a resting place in our Father. His arms are strong and we can find comfort and peace in them. His yoke is easy, and His burdens are light (Matthew 11:30). He is a burden bearer and a shelter from the storms of life. He is a hiding place when the enemy tries to destroy your goals and aspirations. A place in Him is greater than any place bought by man. You will find rest here for your body and your soul. You cannot find rest and trust in man because they are restless themselves. So face today with a smile on your face.

February 22

"Come now, let us reason together, says the LORD: though your sins are like scarlet, they shall be as white as snow; though they are red like crimson, they shall become like wool." Isaiah 1:18, ESV

Come quickly, sister. Let us talk this matter over before you walk away from the protection of our Father. Our Father will discuss this trouble with you, and you will learn the cause of your distress. He is able to forgive your wrongs and wipe them out from the Book of Deeds as if they never happened. Come now and speak to Him. Has He not said that when our wrong acts are red and visible from afar that He will change them and make them white as snow? Go and enter into His grace and mercy. Let Him forgive and comfort you during this troubling time in your life. Our Father is faithful and does not want us to perish.

February 23

To the contrary, "If your enemy is hungry, feed him; if he is thirsty, give him something to drink; for by so doing you will heap burning coals on his head." Romans 12:20, ESV

This enemy has been on your trail for years and will not give up. Stop letting her ride your back. Slay this enemy with love so she will not vex you again. Feed her if she is hungry. Give her water if she is thirsty. Give her clothes when she is naked. These acts of kindness will catch her off guard. She is looking for you to respond to her ways by exchanging evil for evil. She does not know that you are showing her how to forgive and love those who do you wrong. Go into this day with a forgiving heart. The person who was once your enemy will soon be your neighbor and a true friend.

February 24

There is therefore now no condemnation for those who are in Christ Jesus. Romans 8:1, ESV

Daughter, as long as you remain in me, and I in you, no one can show disapproval or criticize you for any of your actions or the words that fall from your lips. In you are the virtues that all men must live by if they seek eternal life. You live by the love that I have planted in your heart. The strength you show is a result of the joy you have in me. Your faith is strong because you see beyond the present time. You see evidence of the things hoped for because they appear before your eyes. You are my beloved daughter in whom I am well pleased for your faithfulness. Walk in my light, and blessings will outpour.

February 25

My people who are called by my name humble themselves, and pray and seek my face and turn from their wicked ways, then I will hear from heaven and will forgive their sin and heal their land.
2 Chronicles 7:14, ESV

Daughter, I see the suffering of my people and I want to reach out and comfort them, but they continue to have the stiff-necked and arrogant behavior as they showed in the wilderness. Their obedience and love for me is short-lived. My heart is heavy for the few remnant who are humble and respect my statutes. I promise not to hurt them. Their prayers are heard and will be answered. They shall live to see this crisis through. However, the masses are stiff-necked and refuse to obey my statutes. The world shall know that I am Lord of all people. When they are fully punished, the land will be healed, and the people will worship me as they did in the land of Canaan. Walk bravely into this day as a warrior who has overcome temptation and the wiles of the devil.

February 26

Hear my prayer, O LORD; let my cry come to you! Do not hide your face from me in the day of my distress! Incline your ear to me; answer me speedily in the day when I call! Psalm 102:1-2, ESV

Daughter, I hear your fervent cry. I was there when this spirit of sickness entered your body. I heard the same plea from the Psalmist who suffered the same affliction over two thousand years ago. I reached out to him and healed his body. There is nothing new that I have not heard or seen. I did not hide my face from him; nor will I leave you alone to bear this pain. I am here with you. You are the apple of my eye. I have great victories in your future. Continue to hold fast to your faith and you will gradually feel strength come back within your body. Keep looking up. Your help is on the way. The faithfulness and obedience you have toward me will go a long way in healing your body. You will persevere!

February 27

And whenever you stand praying, forgive, if you have anything against anyone, so that your Father also who is in heaven may forgive you your trespasses. Mark 11:25, ESV

How can you kneel before the throne of grace when you have ought against your sister? You cannot do it and expect our Father to hear and answer your prayers. You must get up, go to your sister, and ask her forgiveness; then you will be in a position to come and kneel before our Father. If she refuses to receive your plea, your Father will not hold you guilty and will release you from this deed. Your Father, who sees the secret things you say and do, will reward you openly. So go into this day with a new heart and a mind to forgive and forget. Keep the evil thoughts toward a person from entering your heart and count your blessings along the way.

February 28

Even though I walk through the valley of the shadow of death, I will fear no evil, for you are with me; your rod and your staff, they comfort me. Psalm 23:4, ESV

Sister, come and listen to David discuss this Confident Nugget. He had many enemies. When he was attending his father's sheep, there were wolves who tried to attack the sheep. As he grew older, his enemies tracked him as an animal. He thinks about the days of his youth when he used his rod and staff to protect the sheep when they are in danger. David used this thoughts to give him strength. He sees God caring for him by using a rod and a staff to keep his enemies away. David is telling us that when we are in trouble, we can think of a time when we had authority over our surroundings and recall how God protected us. The same God who was there to comfort David is here to comfort you when you are in the valley of despair.

February 29

And now, my daughter, do not fear. I will do for you all that you ask, for all my fellow townsmen know that you are a worthy woman.
Ruth 3:11, ESV

You have much integrity, character, and beauty that set you apart from other women. Your inner light shines and brightens the hearts of those upon which your rays of hope and love fall. You have the same qualities as my daughter Ruth. She loved her mother-in-law so much that she was willing to serve her God and follow her people after the death of her husband. So have no fear of this new journey; I will place people in your path who will recognize the strength in you and will provide for all your needs. Go into this day with confidence in your heart and with endless peace in your mind.

MARCH

The Yellow Daffodil Symbolizes:
forgiveness, honesty, rebirth, new beginnings, and happiness.

March 1

But they who wait for the Lord shall renew their strength; they shall mount up with wings like eagles; they shall run and not be weary; they shall walk and not faint. Isaiah 40:31, ESV

Sister, do not be in such a hurry to climb the ladder of success. Wait until you hear from our Father who can see your future. He will give you strength to face your difficulties. Why take this journey alone when you can run and walk with our Father? He will carry you if you faint. So get up and face this day with joy. Our Father will go with you on this journey.

March 2

For whatever was written in former days was written for our instruction, that through endurance and through the encouragement of the Scriptures we might have hope. **Romans 15:4, ESV**

Sister, our Father wants us to know that those verses we read in the Scriptures were written for us so that when we face similar trials in our own lives, we will know how to overcome them. They are written to show us that if these people conquered their problems and had the strength to endure in spite of odds against them, we too, can endure. These verses will give us hope and will encourage us when we feel like giving up. So rise up, sister. There is hope for your future.

March 3

*The L*ORD *your God is in your midst, a mighty one who will save; he will rejoice over you with gladness; he will quiet you by his love; he will exult over you with loud singing. Zephaniah 3:17, ESV*

Look no further, dear. Here I am. I have been right here in your midst all the time. I have watched you laugh, and my heart was saddened when you cried. I am always here to comfort you when you are alone and when your heart is broken. My love for you is always fresh and will surround you with gladness and joy. I will lift you up out of your valleys of despair, wrap you in my arms, and love you as a father should love his princess. So skip into this day with me watching and guiding your every step. I will never take my eyes off you or leave you alone.

March 4

So Sarah laughed to herself, saying, "After I am worn out, and my lord is old, shall I have pleasure?" Genesis 18:12, ESV

Never doubt my words, daughter. Happiness and bliss can be yours even at your age. All things are possible for anyone who believes in miracles. Remember, Sarah was ninety years of age when she had Isaac. If I can cause her to have pleasure and a son at her age, will I not do the same for you? I am your Father and because you are my daughter, all things are possible if you just believe. Go forth into this day with joy and believe that you will have those things you only dream about. You are as young as you wish to be in your mind. I am faithful to those who are my followers. Even the father of your children knows my faithfulness; he has tried me and found that my words never come back empty or void.

March 5

May the God of hope fill you with all joy and peace in believing, so that by the power of the Holy Spirit you may abound in hope.
Romans 15:13, ESV

Daughter, I have filled you with the gifts of the Holy Spirit so that you may have hope instead of fear and despair. You will have joy when you go through struggles, trials, and oppositions. Love will follow you wherever you walk. It will lead you into paths of righteousness and will cover you when you stand before those in authority. There is peace within you to calm you when anxiety, pain, and trouble enter your heart. Faith will help you to call things that are not seen into things that are seen. Hope will be your gateway to greatness. Without hope, all things good are lost. I will never leave you hopeless or alone.

March 6

You are altogether beautiful, my love; there is no flaw in you.
Song of Solomon 4:7, ESV

Your beauty is deeper than your outer appearance, child. It is on the inside and it radiates outward like a shining star. You are one of my beautiful creations. Your glow is so powerful that it captures the very essence of peace. People are drawn into your beauty and want to be a part of it. Your appearance invites joy, comfort, and happiness. You are an example of my handiwork and you model it very well. Enter into this day with goodness and peace showering you as you meet those who know no peace. Your beauty will captivate their hearts and turn their sadness into happiness. You are an ambassador of my love, peace, and joy. So walk proudly with dignity and honor.

March 7

Charm is deceitful, and beauty is vain, but a woman who fears the LORD is to be praised. Proverbs 31:30, ESV

Sister, there are some women who are impressed with enticing others with their charm and beauty. It is cunning and arrogant for us to behave in such manners. Our Father did not create us to allure men for our comfort. He formed us to be a beacon to show the world the beauty of living for Christ. Our Father's desire is that we will not be ashamed of our inward beauty but to show others grace. When we fear our Father for his majesty, greatness, and righteous judgment, He and the world will praise us for truth and our integrity. So go forth with inward beauty that will change the hearts and minds of women bound with deceit and vanity.

March 8

Let no corrupting talk come out of your mouths, but only such as is good for building up, as fits the occasion, that it may give grace to those who hear. Ephesians 4:29, ESV

Sister, come quick. Here is a Grace Nugget our Father wants us to give to His followers. It is fitting that we do not become double-tongued, talking to believers and nonbelievers about the love of our Father in public, but tearing them down when we are alone. Our mission is to build up the Body of Christ by encouraging others to work for the kingdom of God so they may have grace and mercy at the close of the day when He calls them home. So go forth showing the mercy and grace of our Father. He is a jealous God, but slow to anger. He does not like for us to place any god before Him.

March 9

And after you have suffered a little while, the God of all grace, who has called you to his eternal glory in Christ, will himself restore, confirm, strengthen, and establish you. 1 Peter 5:10, ESV

Daughter, I feel your pain and misery. I am aware of your suffering. I am hurting too, because I saw the disobedience shown toward me when you broke your promise to me. You must endure until my grace flourishes within you and make you whole again. You are going through a time in which you are blaming yourself. There is unrest in your heart. My grace will not enter where there is no peace. Calm yourself by resting in my love. I have not left you alone to bear this burden. I am ready to restore your strength, confidence, and place in the kingdom of daughters who desire to honor and obey my statutes. Go gladly into this day telling others of the love and grace that I offer.

March 10

All glorious is the princess in her chamber, with robes interwoven with gold. Psalm 45:13, ESV

Men of the earth, stand aside and make way for my daughter. I have prepared and dressed her in grace, love, and joy. Her robe is trimmed in refined gold that covers her head down to her feet. She walks in beauty and her steps are ordered according to my precepts. She smells like the blossoms from the Lily of the Valley and the petals from the Rose of Sharon. She is filled with special gifts that show that she is a branch growing from the True Vine which is Jesus Christ. She does not know the evil ways of the world or strive to be a part of it. Honor and respect her for what she represents and who she is. So, daughter, go into this day walking and talking as the princess that you were taught to be. I will supply all your needs according to my riches in glory.

March 11

In the same way, let your light shine before others, so that they may see your good works and give glory to your Father who is in heaven.
Matthew 5:16, ESV

Sister, you need to stop hiding your gifts. Our Father is not pleased with that. He has created you as a shining light to go before His people to share His word with them. When you hide His words, the enemy is happy. His main goal is to enter the hearts and minds of believers and try to sway them away from our Father. You must stand your ground, be strong in our Father's words, and go take the position that He has given you. We have a duty to carry out on the battlefield of life so others may see our good works and glorify our Father in heaven. Let your light shine so our Father may see it from His throne in heaven. So run into this day with gladness in your feet.

March 12

Show yourself in all respects to be a model of good works, and in your teaching show integrity, dignity, and sound speech that cannot be condemned, so that an opponent may be put to shame, having nothing evil to say about us. Titus 2:7-8, ESV

Sister, come and hear this Integrity Nugget we must observe. As we go about our daily work, we must model ourselves as women chosen by our Father to carry His truth. Being chosen does not mean we have to preach or teach from a pulpit or podium. But it does mean that because we know Him and He knows us, we are also His disciples and must follow Him. We should speak truth in a way that those who hear us will not dare question the validity of our report. When we speak truth with integrity this day, it will bring us peace and joy.

March 13

Let no one despise you for your youth, but set the believers an example in speech, in conduct, in love, in faith, in purity. **1 Timothy 4:12, ESV**

Here is another Wisdom Nugget, sister. Whether you are old or young, let no one intimidate you by questioning the authority in which you speak truth. Your truth comes from our Father and the Holy Spirit who live within you. Let them be put to shame for trying to suppress you because of your age. Conduct yourself in such a way that they will be amazed and astonished at the words of wisdom that fall from your lips. So go into this day with confidence that whatever you say, your Father has already approved and sealed it.

March 14

Do not be conformed to this world, but be transformed by the renewal of your mind, that by testing you may discern what is the will of God, what is good and acceptable and perfect. Romans 12:2, ESV

Sister, you cannot be a part of this world or even try to change yourself to fit in it. You were chosen as a daughter to be in the world but not of the world. No one can continue to be hot or cold at the same time while speaking the words of our Father. It is like a two-headed animal. He will spew them out of His mouth because this is a lukewarm person. Your mission is to change the hearts and minds of people back to our Father by offering them eternal life through Jesus Christ. Because you are stronger and persistent in your ways, they were not meant to change you. You know your Father's precepts. He taught them to you so you would not forget them. So greet this day with wisdom and understanding. Your Father will give you discernment to know His will and to do His will.

March 15

The one who rejects me and does not receive my words has a judge; the word that I have spoken will judge him on the last day.
John 12:48, ESV

Listen to this Judgment Nugget, sister. Our Father says that anyone who refuses to hear our words and turn from Him to serve other gods will be judged in the final day. The same words they disregard will be used against them in the judgment. We must be careful to speak truth and honesty as we tell others about our Father and the love and mercy that He has available to them. Let us go into this day with a willing mind to fill the ears of those who will listen so they will not be lost on their final day of earth.

March 16

Whatever you do, work heartily, as for the Lord and not for men, knowing that from the Lord you will receive the inheritance as your reward. You are serving the Lord Christ. Colossians 3:23-24, ESV

Come, here is another Inheritance Nugget. Sister, we must work as if it is our last day to receive this nugget. This is one we really need to put in our box of blessings from our Father. There is one important thing we must remember: The work we do is not earthly work, but it is kingdom building work. This kind of work is not done to receive money. It is building the kingdom of God by bringing souls to His altar of grace. Our Father will reward us if we remain faithful in serving His Son, Jesus Christ. So, sister, we will enter this day prepared to work in our Father's kingdom. When we work for the kingdom, we are also working for the future and for the lives of our children. This is the legacy and inheritance we will leave for them.

March 17

For God will bring every deed into judgment, with every secret thing, whether good or evil. Ecclesiastes 12:14, ESV

Sister, never think that you can hide anything from our Father; He sees all and knows all. It is better to bring anything done in secret before Him and allow Him to pass judgment on you. Trying to hide it from Him will only cause you more hurt and pain. So release the thing that is hidden. To hold onto it in your heart and mind will only bring damnation to your soul in the day of judgment. Our Father is faithful to forgive and will cast the hidden deed in a sea of forgetfulness, never to bring it up again. So greet this day with a renewed mind and soul. Rejoice and be exceedingly glad, for great is your reward in heaven.

March 18

Then he dreamed another dream and told it to his brothers and said, "Behold, I have dreamed another dream. Behold, the sun, the moon, and eleven stars were bowing down to me." Genesis 37:9, ESV

Sister, do not throw your dreams away. It may take a long time, but keep trusting our Father and they will come to pass. Remember, Joseph's brothers called him the dreamer. He dreamed that the sun, moon, and eleven stars bowed down to him. His father rebuked him and said that he, his mother, and eleven brothers would never bow to him. His brothers were jealous and plotted to kill him. They sold him to a caravan of Midianites on their way to Egypt. Well, after twenty years, they all bowed down to him in Egypt where he was second in charge to the king. So you see, your dreams may take years, but our father is faithful. No matter how long it takes, he never forgets His promises. Never give up on your dreams; and most importantly, never give up on our Father.

March 19

No temptation has overtaken you that is not common to man. God is faithful, and he will not let you be tempted beyond your ability, but with the temptation he will also provide the way of escape, that you may be able to endure it. 1 Corinthians 10:13, ESV

Sister, come and listen to this Endurance Nugget. There is no earthly desire or entanglement that our Father is not aware of; He will not allow it to overcome you. He knows your comings and your goings as well as when you lay down and when you get up. Nothing escapes His eyes and ears. He will give you the willpower to endure temptation, no matter what it is. He will also provide a way of escape that will not cause grief or harm to your body. Our Father is faithful and will do exactly what He says He will do. So arise and greet this day with confidence that no matter what comes your way, you will have the endurance to survive. He will give you the added faith and the added strength to overcome your difficulties.

March 20

It is better to take refuge in the LORD than to trust in man.
Psalm 118:8, ESV

Sister, when you are tired, weary, and there is no place to go, you can always find a resting place in our Father. His arms are strong and we can find comfort and peace in them. His yoke is easy, and His burdens are light (Matthew 11:30). He is a burden bearer and a shelter from the storms of life. He is a hiding place when the enemy tries to destroy your goals and aspirations. A place in Him is greater than any place bought by man. You will find rest here for your body and your soul. You cannot find rest and trust in man because they are restless themselves. So face today with a smile on your face.

March 21

"Come now, let us reason together, says the LORD: though your sins are like scarlet, they shall be as white as snow; though they are red like crimson, they shall become like wool." Isaiah 1:18, ESV

Come quickly, sister. Let us talk this matter over before you walk away from the protection of our Father. Our Father will discuss this trouble with you, and you will learn the cause of your distress. He is able to forgive your wrongs and wipe them out from the Book of Deeds as if they never happened. Come now and speak to Him. Has He not said that when our wrong acts are red and visible from afar that He will change them and make them white as snow? Go and enter into His grace and mercy. Let Him forgive and comfort you during this troubling time in your life. Our Father is faithful and does not want us to perish.

March 22

To the contrary, "If your enemy is hungry, feed him; if he is thirsty, give him something to drink; for by so doing you will heap burning coals on his head." Romans 12:20, ESV

This enemy has been on your trail for years and will not give up. Stop letting her ride your back. Slay this enemy with love so she will not vex you again. Feed her if she is hungry. Give her water if she is thirsty. Give her clothes when she is naked. These acts of kindness will catch her off guard. She is looking for you to respond to her ways by exchanging evil for evil. She does not know that you are showing her how to forgive and love those who do you wrong. Go into this day with a forgiving heart. The person who was once your enemy will soon be your neighbor and a true friend.

March 23

There is therefore now no condemnation for those who are in Christ Jesus. Romans 8:1, ESV

Daughter, as long as you remain in me, and I in you, no one can show disapproval or criticize you for any of your actions or the words that fall from your lips. In you are the virtues that all men must live by if they seek eternal life. You live by the love that I have planted in your heart. The strength you show is a result of the joy you have in me. Your faith is strong because you see beyond the present time. You see evidence of the things hoped for because they appear before your eyes. You are my beloved daughter in whom I am well pleased for your faithfulness. Walk in my light, and blessings will outpour.

March 24

If my people who are called by my name humble themselves, and pray and seek my face and turn from their wicked ways, then I will hear from heaven and will forgive their sin and heal their land.
2 Chronicles 7:14, ESV

Daughter, I see the suffering of my people and I want to reach out and comfort them, but they continue to have the stiff-necked and arrogant behavior as they showed in the wilderness. Their obedience and love for me is short-lived. My heart is heavy for the few remnant who are humble and respect my statutes. I promise not to hurt them. Their prayers are heard and will be answered. They shall live to see this crisis through. However, the masses are stiff-necked and refuse to obey my statutes. The world shall know that I am Lord of all people. When they are fully punished, the land will be healed, and the people will worship me as they did in the land of Canaan. Walk bravely into this day as a warrior who has overcome temptation and the wiles of the devil.

March 25

Hear my prayer, O LORD; let my cry come to you! Do not hide your face from me in the day of my distress! Incline your ear to me; answer me speedily in the day when I call! **Psalm 102:1-2, ESV**

Daughter, I hear your fervent cry. I was there when this spirit of sickness entered your body. I heard the same plea from the Psalmist who suffered the same affliction over two thousand years ago. I reached out to him and healed his body. There is nothing new that I have not heard or seen. I did not hide my face from him; nor will I leave you alone to bear this pain. I am here with you. You are the apple of my eye. I have great victories in your future. Continue to hold fast to your faith and you will gradually feel strength come back within your body. Keep looking up. Your help is on the way. The faithfulness and obedience you have toward me will go a long way in healing your body. You will persevere!

March 26

And whenever you stand praying, forgive, if you have anything against anyone, so that your Father also who is in heaven may forgive you your trespasses. Mark 11:25, ESV

How can you kneel before the throne of grace when you have ought against your sister? You cannot do it and expect our Father to hear and answer your prayers. You must get up, go to your sister, and ask her forgiveness; then you will be in a position to come and kneel before our Father. If she refuses to receive your plea, your Father will not hold you guilty and will release you from this deed. Your Father, who sees the secret things you say and do, will reward you openly. So go into this day with a new heart and a mind to forgive and forget. Keep the evil thoughts toward a person from entering your heart and count your blessings along the way.

March 27

Even though I walk through the valley of the shadow of death, I will fear no evil, for you are with me; your rod and your staff, they comfort me. Psalm 23:4, ESV

Sister, come and listen to David discuss this Confident Nugget. He had many enemies. When he was attending his father's sheep, there were wolves who tried to attack the sheep. As he grew older, his enemies tracked him as an animal. He thinks about the days of his youth when he used his rod and staff to protect the sheep when they are in danger. David used this thoughts to give him strength. He sees God caring for him by using a rod and a staff to keep his enemies away. David is telling us that when we are in trouble, we can think of a time when we had authority over our surroundings and recall how God protected us. The same God who was there to comfort David is here to comfort you when you are in the valley of despair.

March 28

And now, my daughter, do not fear. I will do for you all that you ask, for all my fellow townsmen know that you are a worthy woman.
Ruth 3:11, ESV

You have much integrity, character, and beauty that set you apart from other women. Your inner light shines and brightens the hearts of those upon which your rays of hope and love fall. You have the same qualities as my daughter Ruth. She loved her mother-in-law so much that she was willing to serve her God and follow her people after the death of her husband. So have no fear of this new journey; I will place people in your path who will recognize the strength in you and will provide for all your needs. Go into this day with confidence in your heart and with endless peace in your mind.

March 29

__Do not lie to one another, seeing that you have put off the old self with its practices. Colossians 3:9, ESV__

Being untruthful to others indicates that you have gone back to your old ways. This is not acceptable with our Father. If you want to be His daughter, your ways must change. So amend your practices and He will open His arms and welcome you as He has done before. Confess the things you have done wrong to Him and He will forgive.

March 30

An excellent wife who can find? She is far more precious than jewels.
Proverbs 31:10, ESV

Sister, be chaste and stay away from evil men. A good man wants a virtuous woman who is full of wisdom, kindness, and faithfulness. Never go looking for a man, because you will find more than what you ask for. So keep yourself pure and above reproach. Our Father will reward you for your faithfulness and send you a good man after His own heart.

March 31

And Pharisees came up and in order to test him asked, "Is it lawful for a man to divorce his wife?" Mark 10:2, ESV

Sister, why worry yourself about this matter? Matthew's gospel says the only reason you may leave your husband is for immorality. That is why Moses gave men a bill of divorcement to save women from danger. If your husband asks forgiveness, you must forgive and continue in love. There will be no marriages in heaven. So go into this day keeping our Father's statutes. He will reward you for your obedience and count you as a loving and devoted daughter.

APRIL

The Dogwood Bloom Symbolizes:
rebirth, resurrection, life, purity, affection, strength, and new beginnings

April 1

Knowing this first of all, that no prophecy of Scripture comes from someone's own interpretation. 2 Peter 1:20, ESV

Sister, no one can predict the future from reading the word of God unless they have been born of the Spirit. How can someone point you to the way of Christ when they do not know Him or observe His ways? Trust His words and your belief in Him. You know Him because He is in you and you are in Him. So go into today teaching, living, and showing spiritual truth.

April 2

*Oh, taste and see that the L*ORD *is good! Blessed is the man who takes refuge in him! Psalm 34:8, ESV*

Sister, come and rest in our Father's arms. Taste and see that He is good. He is food when we are hungry. He is the Bread of Life that feeds us with the word. He is the True Vine from which we drink the wine of rebirth and regeneration. He is water that refreshes our souls, which causes us to never thirst again. So go joyfully into this day with the birth of hope, peace, and a new beginning.

April 3

And I will make of you a great nation, and I will bless you and make your name great, so that you will be a blessing. Genesis 12:2, ESV

Daughter, I have great plans in store for you. You have been faithful and patient when trials came to disrupt your life. You held on in spite of disappointments, pain, turmoil, and disorder. Because you have placed your life on hold, there is a reward awaiting you. Although there were times when it seemed that you would fold, you kept the faith. Your name will be known by many people who will come to hear you impart wisdom and knowledge. You will be a blessing to those who hear your words. So get up and start to begin to live. The future awaits your coming.

April 4

And she saw two angels in white, sitting where the body of Jesus had lain, one at the head and one at the feet. John 20:12, ESV

Mary Magdalene looked into the tomb and saw two angels standing at the tomb of Jesus. They asked, "Why do you look for the living among the dead? He is not here; he has risen!" (Luke 24:5-6, BSB). Can you imagine the joy that raced through her heart when she heard that her Savior had risen from the grave? That is good news, sister, for all believers. It is good news because He has taken our sins and all the sins of the world and buried them in the tomb when He arose. Now we are free from the laws of bondage. We have become heirs with Him and can claim possessions in His will and testament. That lets us know that if we are in Christ when we die, we shall rise from the grave just as He did. Rise and walk into this day with victory over death and the grave. Your Father has given you an eternal gift of life. Cherish it and it will carry you forward.

April 5

No one born of God makes a practice of sinning, for God's seed abides in him; and he cannot keep on sinning, because he has been born of God. 1 John 3:9, ESV

Sister, because we are in Christ and He is in us, we cannot continue to do wrong. His seeds have been planted deep within our hearts and minds. As the seeds sprout from a seedling to a large tree, our faith in Him should also grow in us. As the tree grows with branches, our families grow, and the faith is transferred from us to them. We do not want to see them do wrong. We have been taught truth and righteousness, and we are born again. So greet this day with a new spirit and a new desire to do right, even in distressful times.

April 6

For the time is coming when people will not endure sound teaching, but having itching ears they will accumulate for themselves teachers to suit their own passions. 2 Timothy 4:3, ESV

Sister, do not be alarmed when people are changing before your eyes. They will believe one thing today, but will say you are wrong tomorrow because their ears like the sound of teaching that is not sound and built on a God-fearing foundation. Do not get caught up in their practices of looking for teachers who will say what they want to hear. Just be yourself and ignore them by loving them from a distance. Teach what you know to be true. Teach what your Father has taught you. Finally, above all things, teach what you feel is in your heart. So go joyfully into this day. Remove all the negative thoughts from your mind and flow with positive thoughts. Your Father is pleased with your respect for the true word and your defense of it. He will be with you as you teach truth and righteousness.

April 7

I have been crucified with Christ. It is no longer I who live, but Christ who lives in me. And the life I now live in the flesh I live by faith in the Son of God, who loved me and gave himself for me.
Galatians 2:20, ESV

Sister, I know it is hard to live right when many who surround you are not in our Father. That is why you must preserve and keep the word hidden in your heart so you can say to them when adversity comes your way, "For I know that nothing good dwells in me, that is, in my flesh" (Romans 7:18, ESV), because from it comes issues that conflict with the spirit of truth and righteousness. I know you are going through indecisiveness in your body and spirit. Our Father said that because of the flesh and its weaknesses, He will not place anything upon us that we cannot bear. So go forth into this day with the cross of salvation ahead of you as a reminder of what our Lord has sacrificed for your freedom from bondage and the grave.

April 8

Therefore, if anyone is in Christ, he is a new creation. The old has away; behold, the new has come. 2 Corinthians 5:17, ESV

Sister, you were made a new person through Jesus Christ when you accepted Him as your Lord and Savior. Many of your friends may not understand your ways or how you talk and think differently. Some will even ignore you and slowly leave your side. But do not be discouraged, your Father will place people in your path who will have the same newness that you now experience. So fear not as you approach this day. There is a new life and a new purpose awaiting you. Just be a willing vessel and allow it to work inside of you.

April 9

May he give you the desire of your heart and make all your plans succeed. Psalm 20:4, NIV

All your hopes and dreams will come to pass because I have ordained and declared them to happen within your season. Your season is quickly approaching and you must begin to prepare for its arrival. Daughter, you are special to me. You have worked hard to provide for your livelihood and you take care to see that those who are less fortunate are secure and safe. There are very few daughters like you who place others above their own needs. I have observed you over the years and found you to be a compassionate and caring daughter. I will reward you openly for your faithfulness. So walk into your season of health, blessings, and prosperity.

April 10

Blessed be the God and Father of our Lord Jesus Christ! According to his great mercy, he has caused us to be born again to a living hope through the resurrection of Jesus Christ from the dead.
1 Peter 1:3, ESV

Daughter, you are blessed beyond measure. You have a right to all the riches in glory, the things you desire in your goals, and the plans you have worked for. You have chosen to live your life in me and you have a living hope. My Son has given His life for you when He died on the cross. Cast all your burdens and cares upon me. You can receive a rebirth of faith and hope that all the things you speak will come into existence. Run faithfully into this day. Run with joy, beauty, and love for life. My grace and mercy will always be running alongside you.

April 11

*And he said, "May you be blessed by the L*ORD*, my daughter. You have made this last kindness greater than the first in that you have not gone after young men, whether poor or rich." Ruth 3:10, ESV*

Come quickly and listen to this Love Nugget; Boaz is proposing to Ruth. She has been faithful to Naomi, her mother-in-law, and our Father. Boaz sees wonderful qualities in her because she did not run after other men while she was with Naomi. Sister, a daughter's integrity speaks volumes about her character. If you want a Boaz in your life, you must be faithful to your Father and wait for Him to place the right man in your life. So go into today praising our Father for sending your Boaz to love and care for you. If you already have a mate, our Father will touch him so he will become your Boaz in his mind, body, and soul.

April 12

Whatever you do, work at it with all your heart, as working for the Lord, not for human masters, since you know that you will receive an inheritance from the Lord as a reward. It is the Lord Christ you are serving. Colossians 3:23-24, NIV

Sister, whatever task you are asked to perform, whether it is in keeping with your job or with the spiritual work you have been called to do, let it be done in love. There may be times when you feel discouraged, but hold your peace. In doing so, you will please your Father. Your Father sees all and is keeping record just like those over you. He knows that your work is not to please men, but to serve Him faithfully. He will reward you openly for your service. He said that we are to serve those who are overseers and in charge of our work. So greet this day with love in your heart. Your reward is waiting at the close of the day.

April 13

They replied, "Believe in the Lord Jesus, and you will be saved—you and your household." Acts 16:31, NIV

Sister, here is a Salvation Nugget that Apostle Paul wants you to share as you meet believers and nonbelievers on your journey. He taught many people about the love of our Father and how they can be saved. It is important that everyone knows that when they accept Jesus Christ as their Lord and Savior, not only will they be saved, but their entire household will be saved too. If anyone asks you the meaning of being saved, tell them it is escaping the wrath of our Father. No one wants to be the object of His wrath, because that is when He applies His vengeance upon the unrighteous. So go into today spreading the good news to all who will believe on Him.

April 14

Let love and faithfulness never leave you; bind them around your neck, write them on the tablet of your heart. Then you will win favor and a good name in the sight of God and man. Proverbs 3:3-4, NIV

Daughter, never let love and faithfulness leave your heart and thoughts. These are the things that win favor with me and others. When people see the love in your heart, they will cherish you. When they witness the faith by which you believe as you climb impossible mountains and cross deep and treacherous waters, they will admire your determination. These are traits that will bring praise upon my name and assure you a place in the kingdom. So go forth with my blessings. You have won my favor and trust. I will place angels before you to guard your footsteps as you walk in paths of righteousness for my name's sake.

April 15

*Trust in the L*ORD *with all your heart, and do not lean on your own understanding. In all your ways acknowledge him, and he will make straight your paths.* Proverbs 3:5-6, ESV

Sister, it is not good to give our opinions on matters of the heart or soul without discussing them with our Father. When we answer out of our flesh rather than the Spirit of our Father, we may cause great harm and danger to a believer who is new in Christ. When we trust our Father with our hearts, minds, and souls, we will not speak without grace and mercy in our tone of voice. We must let believers know that these are not our words that we speak, but the words of our Father. Your Father loves you and has taught you His precepts and laws. He wants you to succeed in every task you have assigned yourself to achieve. So greet this day with gladness and joy that you are walking in a straight path made by your Father.

April 16

For I am with you, and no one is going to attack and harm you, because I have many people in this city. **Acts 18:10, NIV**

Daughter, have no fear of what lies ahead of you. Put those thoughts out of your mind. You are already covered under my wings of protection. I know that this is a new road and journey you have taken. But just like I was with my servant Paul, I promise to be with you. You may not see me, but I will be in the hearts and minds of the people I will place in your path. No one will harm you or cause you grief. They will know from your walk, talk, and attitude that you are the daughter of a King. So go forth with wings of mercy guarding your thoughts and lips that the words you speak will be pure, clean, and forceful in my love.

April 17

One night the Lord spoke to Paul in a vision: Do not be afraid; keep on speaking, do not be silent. Acts 18:9, NIV

Have you ever had a vision of our Father, an angel, or a person you know standing before you? Were they giving you a warning or showing you things that that will happen in the future? Do not fear these visits. They have happened before to other people. They come to give you strength, courage, and to assure you that whatever happens in your future, you will be fine. They come to make you aware of what is about to take place so you will know your place in the event. So go into today with confidence "that all things work together for the good of those who love God, who are called according to his purpose" (Romans 8:28, CSB). Consider yourself blessed to have this gift. There is a reason our Father chose to give you this gift, so use it for His purpose.

April 18

But in your hearts revere Christ as Lord. Always be prepared to give an answer to everyone who asks you to give the reason for the hope that you have. But do this with gentleness and respect. 1 Peter 3:15, ESV

Daughter, never be afraid to defend your faith and the words of your Father. There will be many nonbelievers who will question your hope. They will deny my very existence, my power to heal, and my ability to give life to those in despair. Be consistent in your answer and always give a word of kindness. Respect their positions, but do not bow down to them. They are not your god. I am your God, your Father, and your deliverer. So get up and greet this day with a triumphant spirit and renewed faith. I am supreme and have sovereignty over all the earth. You will be rewarded for your faithfulness.

April 19

Let us fix our eyes on Jesus, the author and perfecter of our faith, who for the joy set before Him endured the cross, scorning its shame, and sat down at the right hand of the throne of God. Hebrews 12:2, BSB

Daughter, I know that there are times that try your spirit and soul. Let not your heart be troubled nor let it be afraid. I did not bring you this far to be destroyed and left behind. Whenever you are troubled and do not know where to turn, look up. When you cannot find a friend to hold your hand, look up. When your money is low and there is no food to eat, look up. Look up and you will feel me looking down upon you. I will never leave or forsake you. You are my princess and my beloved daughter. Continue in my love; for yet in just a little while I will come and bring my reward with me. So go in peace and keep your eyes on my Son. He is your intercessor and will tell me about your needs.

April 20

But understand this, that in the last days there will come times of difficulty. 2 Timothy 3:1, ESV

Daughter, I see the trouble that continually follows you and the difficult times you are having at home and at work. Do not allow these times to get you down. They will last a very short time. Do not be disturbed when you see signs that may cause you to think that the world is at an end. Although it is true that you are living in the last days, the end is not at hand. The same was said in the days of Paul, Titus, and John, but the end came for some as it will for some today. These signs are a warning for all to get ready during these difficult times. The death angel will come for any one of us at any time. Your Father is the only one who knows the end time.

April 21

You need to persevere so that when you have done the will of God, you will receive what he has promised. Hebrew 10:36, NIV

Precious child, you have worked far beyond what is required of you. I know you have a heart filled with love and care, but you are only one person, so you need to rest. You are persistent and believe in doing your best at any task assigned. There is a reward awaiting you at the close of the day. Your work is above reproach and this kind of work will always be here. The kind of work that you must never give up on is showing nonbelievers the way to the cross. When you have done this work, there will be a crown awaiting you in glory. So as you perform both types of work, know that I am pleased and will send countless blessings your way.

April 22

Sometimes you were publicly exposed to insult and persecution; at other times you stood side by side with those who were so treated.
Hebrews 10:33, NIV

Sister, you have been through so much in such a short time. There have been many enemies who rose up against you, but they fell and did not succeed. Yet, you have kept your strength and character. There have been many people who have been through less and did not survive. Great is your faithfulness. You have a determination to succeed in spite of the odds that were stacked against you. Many people seek your support when they are facing similar problems in their lives. They have witnessed your fortitude and courage. They admire you for your convictions and faith in what you believe.

April 23

You shall be a crown of beauty in the hand of the LORD, and a royal diadem in the hand of your God. Isaiah 62:3, ESV

Our Father has showered you with beauty and favor. You are a symbol of authority in His eyes. Your radiant character sparkles as a diamond sending rays of light upon those in its path. Your voice is like the sound of rushing waters falling from a cliff with majesty, force, and drawing power. Count it all joy, sister. Your Father is carrying you in His hands. You have advanced so much in your profession that He has found favor in you. He will protect you from danger with the covering of His wings. Go swiftly into this day with love, goodness, and mercy following you all the days of your life.

April 24

He drew me up from the pit of destruction, out of the miry bog, and set my feet upon a rock, making my steps secure. **Psalm 40:2, ESV**

Our Father is "no respecter of persons" (Acts 10:34, KJV). What He has done for one person, He will do the same for another. It does not matter what station a woman finds herself in life, where she lives, or where she comes from. He has given so many people a second, third, and seventy times seven chances. That is the kind of Father He is, and the kind of God we serve. He will pull you out of the muck and miry mud and place your feet on a solid foundation. Then He will give you all the tools you will need to start over. He will even place people around you to give you a fresh start. He will in no wise turn anyone away. His desire is to make you feel safe and secure. So run and tell all your friends that our Father will welcome them into the fold.

April 25

There is no fear in love, but perfect love casts out fear. For fear has to do with punishment, and whoever fears has not been perfected in love.
1 John 4:18, ESV

Do you know what true love is all about? Do you know what it means to love in spite of? True love comes from our Father and that same love is given to us when we are in Him. Then, and only then, we can love others as he loves us. He loves us unconditionally, no matter what we have done in the past. That is the kind of love we should have for our spouses, friends, and enemies. This kind of love knows no fear because perfect love casts out all fear. This is what an agape love is all about. It goes beyond passionate love because it is lasting, whereas passionate love will change. So go into tomorrow exercising this agape love.

April 26

For a day in your courts is better than a thousand elsewhere. I would rather be a doorkeeper in the house of my God than dwell in the tents of wickedness. Psalm 84:10, ESV

Never allow the love of wealth, positions, or titles identify you or be the object of your personal possessions. These things will change and tarnish with time. Do not be impressed with houses, buildings, or worldly kingdoms. They will soon fall and crumble to the ground. What looks good on the outside may be a phony show on the inside. Never be too proud to sweep a floor, pick up paper, or feed a sick person. These things are steppingstones to good health, prosperity, and righteousness. The doorkeeper is the lowly position in any organization. It is better to be an usher in the house of our Father than to sit in a castle where there is wickedness. So go into this day with peace and joy following you.

April 27

The grass withers, the flower fades, but the word of our God will stand forever. Isaiah 40:8, ESV

Sister, here is a Beauty Nugget you must listen to. Never think or believe that beauty belongs to certain people. True beauty is how a person looks upon you. Some may look on the outside while others look deep within the heart and soul. Inner beauty lasts forever. Everything that is alive will one day grow old, fade away, and die. But, sister, our Father's words that bloom from His mouth will never fade away or die. They will live forever, even after beauty has left this world. That is why He wants us to hide His words in our hearts. The day is rapidly approaching when we will not have the Holy Bible to read as we do now. Evil men will seek to destroy our Father's word. But as long as we have it in our hearts, we can still enjoy the peace and comfort it brings us.

April 28

She is a tree of life to those who take hold of her; those who hold her fast will be blessed. Proverbs 3:18, NIV

Daughter, learn much from mother wisdom. Never forsake her or turn away from her. Her roots and vines are a source of life's substances of truth, healing, and blessings. Her leaves are strength and courage for the weary. Take a firm hold of her and never let go of her. She is a mother to all who seek understanding. She will cover and give you shade from the scorching heat of the oppressor. Trust her to lead you into paths of righteousness. Your hold on wisdom will be greater than silver and you will profit more personal gain than gold. So go forth into this day with blessings. The shadows of wisdom will forever follow you.

April 29

For I will give you a mouth and wisdom, which none of your adversaries will be able to withstand or contradict. Luke 21:15, ESV

Daughter, stop worrying about the things in which you have no control. You should know that when you open your mouth it is I who speak for you. The thoughts you ponder in your mind comes from me. I have been with you all this time. Why would I leave you now? Have I not given you words to speak that have caused nonbelievers to hide in shame? Then there was the time when your enemies came against you to destroy you with words of distrust and I placed words of confidence and strength in your mouth to overcome them. I will always be with you when you speak. For out of your mouth will flow words of wisdom and understanding. So daughter, run speedily into this day. My wisdom, knowledge, and understanding will be running gracefully alongside of you.

April 30

Call to me and I will answer you, and will tell you great and hidden things that you have not known. Jeremiah 33:3, ESV

My prophet Jeremiah was a young boy when I called him to prophesy to my people in exile. He will tell you that when he had doubts about his prophecies, all he had to do was call me and I would answer. So, daughter, I am giving you the same ear that I gave Jeremiah. When you have problems or do not know which path to take, call on me and I will answer. I will let you down in the deep treasures of my mind and show you those things that are hidden from evil men and the world. So get up with joy and peace in your heart. You have delighted yourself in me and I will reward you bountifully. Everything you ask of me will be yours to receive.

MAY

The Black-Eyed Susan Symbolizes:
encouragement, patience, broad-mindedness, motivation, and long-suffering

May 1

For I know the plans I have for you, declares the LORD, plans for welfare and not for evil, to give you a future and a hope.
Jeremiah 29:11, ESV

Daughter, you are precious in my sight. I see your work and dedication. You have the heart of my daughter Dorcas, and the determination of my daughter Esther. You are truly my daughter. The unyielding faith and hope you have is above reproach. I know the plans for your future and position in life. I will not allow harm or danger to overcome you. I will provide a way for your escape. So enter today with hope, faith, and love overlooking you and guiding your footsteps.

May 2

Those who sow in tears shall reap with shouts of joy!
Psalm 126:5, ESV

I will dry the tears from your eyes, dear, and place a sparkle in them. These struggles that you are facing now are only temporal. They will not last forever. I know you have worked hard and have not received your earthly reward. But do not grow weary in your waiting. Your weeping will endure for a night, but your joy will come in the morning. Unspeakable joy is on its way. So enter this day with joy and happiness, for you will soon have peace. My ears are not closed where I cannot hear your voice. Your cries have reached my ears.

May 3

Those of steadfast mind you keep in peace—in peace because they trust in you. Trust in the Lord forever, for in the Lord God you have an everlasting rock. Isaiah 26:3-4, NRSV

Sister, you have a stable and a lasting rock in our Father. In times of trouble, strife, confusion, and opposition, you can hide in Him. When your enemies are in pursuit of you, there is a place where you can find shelter and refuge from them. Our Father knows that you trust Him. He feels the love you have for Him. He knows that you are a peacemaker and that many people trust your decisions and choices. He plans to protect you by providing this hiding place for you. So leap into today knowing that there is a place waiting for you to escape where no one will see you or know where you are. Rejoice and be glad.

May 4

I will lead the blind by ways they have not known, along unfamiliar paths I will guide them; I will turn the darkness into light before them and make the rough places smooth. Isaiah 42:16, NIV

Daughter, you have no reason to fear danger or anyone who comes against you. Your way and purpose have already been established. I am here to protect and defend you from evil and impending dangers. I am the light that will guide you through life's processes. I will see everything for you. Your eyes are my eyes. I will allow you to see around corners to identify the enemy before he can overpower you. I am your tower in which you can climb to see danger approaching from afar. I will save you from temptation and the attacks of the enemy. So go gladly into this day with my light shining in the darkness, making your paths clear of upcoming danger. I am a lamp for your paths.

May 5

Let another praise you, and not your own mouth; a stranger, and not your own lips. Proverbs 27:2, ESV

Many people will think highly of you and will carry your name far and near. Some will emulate you and will want to follow in your footsteps. The integrity and character you show is an example of how you model excellence. When you exemplify greatness in your profession and lifestyle, other people will speak for you. They will justify and validate your work, and you need not ever open your mouth. So go into today with confidence. Your renowned reputation goes before you to prepare the way for you.

May 6

Whoever is of God hears the words of God. The reason why you do not hear them is that you are not of God. John 8:47, ESV

Life is not a game of mad gab, which is a game played by people to make sentences of words strewn together in a pile. Words as simple as they are, when placed together in a certain order, can cause grief, anger, joy, or pronounce life and death. Do not allow evil words to announce your destiny nor let anyone speak death over your life. You are my daughter, created and crafted in my image. There is nothing that is withheld from you. The many secrets of the universe have been revealed to you to make your plans come to pass. You have been taught my precepts and you know my will. So greet this day with words of love and words of hope, and in return, you will receive my words to direct your life and lead you to heights of success and prosperity.

May 7

And whatever you ask in prayer, you will receive, if you have faith.
Matthew 21:22, ESV

There is much authority in knowing and exercising the power of faith. The power of faith allows you to hope for things that do not exist and to speak them into existence. The power of faith lets you believe that you already have the things you desire because you see them in your minds. If everyone had the power of faith, they could speak to a crisis and it will leave this world and never come back again. But the key is everyone. Some will believe, then there are many who will not believe. So as you greet today, speak everything you desire into existence that will enhance your life's processes. Start watching your hopes materialize and bring imminent changes into this world.

May 8

For the word of God is living and active, sharper than any two-edged sword, piercing to the division of soul and of spirit, of joints and of marrow, and discerning the thoughts and intentions of the heart.
Hebrews 4:12, ESV

Sister, there will be many who will speak evil of you and spread rumors and lies about your love of life. Leave them alone. Our Father knows their thoughts and what is pondering in their minds. His words are alive and at work when they are not aware that He is in their midst. His words are sharp like a double-edged knife. They can cut through the heart, pierce the soul, and read their thoughts before they form in their minds. That is the kind of God we serve. So go on your way with your head held high. You are your Father's child and no evil will come near you.

May 9

For I am not ashamed of the gospel, for it is the power of God for salvation to everyone who believes, to the Jew first and also to the Greek. Romans 1:16, ESV

Let no one cause you to lower your head in shame of who you are, where you came from, or what you believe. Our Savior, Jesus Christ, who is our Brother in the Spirit, gave His life for our belief and faith in this gospel. He hung on the cross for us and shed His blood so that we may be saved from eternal damnation to our souls. No one who believes in His death and resurrection should be ashamed of the sacrifice He made for us on that old rugged tree. This gospel is free to anyone who will accept it. So go into today with a burst of energy radiating from the power of the gospel of Jesus Christ.

May 10

Whoever believes in me, as the Scripture has said, 'Out of his heart will flow rivers of living water.' John 7:38, ESV

Daughter, I formed you from the dust of the earth and blew the breath of life into your body. Your thoughts are my thoughts. The hopes and dreams you passionately speak about are the ones I have planted in your mind. I have created you from the deep treasures of my mind. There is so much of me in you, and one day my Spirit will issue forth like a living waterfall giving spiritual water to all who will listen and drink from this fountain. Some will not understand your gifts and will refuse to hear them. Do not be discouraged. There will be more who will drink from this fountain than those who will go away thirsty for this water. So leap into today. Rivers of living waters flow within your veins.

May 11

Now the man Moses was very meek, more than all people who were on the face of the earth. Numbers 12:3, ESV

Sister, come and listen to this Meek Nugget. You know the story of Moses and how he had a speech impediment and was afraid to speak to Pharaoh about the mission our Father sent him on. Well, our Father told him to go and that He would speak through him and send his brother Aaron along with him. Although Moses was lacking in conversation, our Father had equipped him with a gentle and caring personality that surpassed all his other weaknesses. So you see, even though we may be lacking in one area, our Father will increase the attribute(s) that will give us success and praise among people. So whatever weakness you may have, prepare yourself to receive a blessing from our Father. He will fix it for you.

May 12

But he was pierced for our transgressions; he was crushed for our iniquities; upon him was the chastisement that brought us peace, and with his wounds we are healed. **Isaiah 53:5, ESV**

Sister, come closer. Here is a Healing Nugget. Our Father wants us to know that there is healing in the public flogging that Christ received. For every stripe of the strap that crushed His body, we were healed of our wounds and pains. These words should bring us consolation and comfort when disease enters our bodies and causes pain. So greet this day by passing this nugget onto others who are suffering from sickness, affliction, or pain. Let them know that their longsuffering will be rewarded for the patience they endured.

May 13

Therefore confess your sins to each other and pray for each other so that you may be healed. The prayer of a righteous person is powerful and effective. James 5:16, NIV

Sister, stay in the company of people who know, love, and serve our Father. When you are in the company of nonbelievers, your heart will feel the rays of discomfort and strife coming from them. Believers have the same heart as you and know the precepts and statutes of our Father. You can talk to them and exchange conversations about the reasons you came to Christ. Not only that, but they can pray with you when you are too weak to pray for yourself. This type of setting will allow you to also bring people to your group who do not know the Father and teach them how to pray and how to forgive others for their wrong actions.

May 14

A joyful heart is good medicine, but a crushed spirit dries up the bones.
Proverbs 17:22, ESV

Make sure your heart is full of joy and love, so that when trials, grief, and struggles come into your life, you will be able to bear them. A heart full of joy is like medicine in your cabinet. It will soothe you and serve as a balm to ease pain and sickness. But a heart filled with anger, haste, and sadness, crushes the spirit and incites rage. The Spirit of our Father cannot move freely in such a place. His Spirit needs room to grow. It needs a place that will invite Him to enter and take control. So go joyfully into today with your heart feeling the medicine of peace, love, and joy. Your Father is pleased with your service.

May 15

Though you have not seen him, you love him. Though you do not now see him, you believe in him and rejoice with joy that is inexpressible and filled with glory. 1 Peter 1:8, ESV

Sister, we have never seen our Father, but we feel His presence and can hear Him speak softly to our ears and throughout our bodies. We do not need to see Him to believe, trust, or know that He is present at all times through our trials and struggles. That is why we love and depend on Him to supply all our needs. We are happy that He hears our cries and comes to our rescue. We realize that we do not deserve a Father like Him, but we freely accept his call of salvation and repentance when we go astray. So approach this day with confidence in knowing that he will be there to guide your steps as you walk.

May 16

*Then he said to them, "Go your way. Eat the fat and drink sweet wine and send portions to anyone who has nothing ready, for this day is holy to our Lord. And do not be grieved, for the joy of the L*ORD *is your strength."* Nehemiah 8:10, ESV

Stop allowing bad news to steal your joy. It is a blessing when you can feel some joy in this world when everything else is falling apart. When Ezra, the priest of Israel, read from the Bible, the people began to cry because they had not heard God speak in years. Ezra boldly declared that the joy of the Lord is responsible for his strength. So get up, run, and praise your Father and stop letting the world steal your joy. Your joy comes from the Holy Spirit. Rejoice, be glad, and receive your joy.

May 17

You make known to me the path of life; in your presence there is fullness of joy; at your right hand are pleasures forevermore.
Psalm 16:11, ESV

Daughter, you are my dew in the morning. The sparkles and freshness in your face just light up any space I place you in. Your persistence and boldness are known in your talk and your walk. You are truly a gift to the world. For as I have taught you about the paths of righteousness, you tell the same to others and place them on the right path to life eternal. You complete my joy. You are full of joyful expressions and spread this joy around to everyone who knows you. So continue in my love and my blessings. Others will be blessed from just knowing you and being in your presence.

May 18

For you shall go out in joy and be led forth in peace; the mountains and the hills before you shall break forth into singing, and all the trees of the field shall clap their hands. Isaiah 55:12, ESV

Daughter, you are the essence of poetry as you walk in beauty and grace. Your character and integrity lead others to peace and comfort. When people of lofty positions come in your presence, there is an air of submission and respect that break forth like songs of joy and adoration. When you speak, the sounds of clapping hands are like showers of water breaking over a waterfall. So go forth into today spreading the joy that has been placed in you. Sow seeds of kindness and you shall reap the harvest of goodness and strength.

May 19

*The L*ORD *is my light and my salvation; whom shall I fear?*
*The L*ORD *is the stronghold of my life; of whom shall I be afraid?*
Psalm 27:1, ESV

Daughter, walk in the light. There is no good thing that will ever come from walking in darkness. So, walk in me, for I am your light where you can see in the spiritual as well as the physical realm. When you walk in the salvation of which you have been saved, the world will see me in you and will fear the words that flow from your mouth. These words will flow like rivers of living waters because I live in you and you live in me. It is I who speak. I am your strong tower. You can climb up in me and look at your enemies to see what they are plotting against you. When they come before you as one, they will scatter as seven spirits when they hear your voice.

May 20

For nothing is hidden that will not be made manifest, nor is anything secret that will not be known and come to light. Luke 8:17, ESV

You can never hide anything of value spoken in secrecy because someone will find it and bring it to the light. If not now, it will come to the light after your death. So live a life above reproach and you will have no fear of secrets hidden in your past. If there are some things that come to the surface, admit them, and clean the slate. Tell them that your Father is your judge and that if He has forgiven you, it matters little what anyone else says. You cannot please everyone all the time. So go forth and pray for the courage of those who are victims of hidden secrets that they may be able to receive forgiveness; the enemy has deceived them in believing that they must live in guilt and condemnation.

May 21

For you formed my inward parts; you knitted me together in my mother's womb. I praise you, for I am fearfully and wonderfully made. Wonderful are your works; my soul knows it very well.
Psalm 139:13-14, ESV

Father, I am so happy that you created me in your image. You formed me while I was yet to be born and gathered all the major ingredients from your field of stardust to make me who I am today. Father, I give you the highest praise. I magnify your name and lift you higher than the highest star in the heavens. You wove the finest human traits together and fearfully created me. You placed your spirit of love, joy, and peace in my heart. It pains me to know that I have caused harm to any one of your creatures. Father, I love you because you first loved me.

May 22

For we aim at what is honorable not only in the Lord's sight but also in the sight of man. 2 Corinthians 8:21, ESV

Sister, cast your hopes and desires on the higher things in life such as honor, trust, and faithfulness. These things will carry you further in life because they are the springboards upon which greatness is launched. Not only will you receive the approval of your Father, but the world will see the good in you and will remember your name. So go forth into tomorrow carrying the badge of courage, honor, and truth. Many people will respect your work and look to you for guidance during these trying times.

May 23

So I always take pains to have a clear conscience toward both God and man. Acts 24:16, ESV

Sister, come quickly and listen to this Conscience Nugget. Always make sure your conscience is clear in all things toward others and especially toward your Father. He knows every thought that enters your mind before you speak them. You may fool man, but you can never fool Him. Apostle Paul wrote this verse because he represented God and he knew that if he was not honest as he dealt with God's people, he had to answer to Him. The same thing applies to you. You represent your employer as well as the people who emulate you. So go into today knowing that what you say and do have consequences.

May 24

*Vindicate me, O L*ORD*, for I have walked in my integrity, and I have trusted in the L*ORD *without wavering. Psalm 26:1, ESV*

Precious child, I see that there are those who wish you harm. They have even spoken false words and caused others to mistrust you. Do not respond by doing evil for evil. Leave them alone and let them hang themselves. "Vengeance is mine, I will repay" them for what they have done to all my servants (Romans 12:19, KJV). Love those who falsely accuse you and do good to those who deceive and misuse you, for great is your reward in heaven. Continue steadfastly in my service. I am running alongside you to vindicate you with my words.

May 25

*And the L*ORD *said to Satan, "Have you considered my servant Job, that there is none like him on the earth, a blameless and upright man, who fears God and turns away from evil? He still holds fast his integrity, although you incited me against him to destroy him without reason." Job 2:3, ESV*

Do not be weary when trouble appears to follow you and you cannot seem to shake it. Look what happened to Job, who was an upright man and did no evil in our Father's sight. Satan wanted to tempt him to see how devoted he was to God. Our Father gave him permission to tempt Job by taking all he had. But, Satan was not allowed to take Job's life. Did you know that Satan asks our Father to tempt us too? Our Father expects us to hold out just like Job. So go peacefully into today. Hold on and hold out. The Lord will provide an escape when temptation is too much to bear.

May 26

Then his wife said to him, "Do you still hold fast your integrity? Curse your God and die." Job 2:9, ESV

Sometimes your honesty and goodness are questioned by those you love because they do not understand your life and the purpose to which you have been called. Just like Job's wife, who was blinded by the loss of everything she had including her children, your loved one will become jealous of your faithfulness to our Father. If you can just hold on and hold out as Job did, your Father will restore all that was lost and more. So greet this day with strength and determination. What the devil has taken, your Father will give it back.

May 27

*The L*ORD *appeared to him from far away. I have loved you with an everlasting love; therefore I have continued my faithfulness to you.*
Jeremiah 31:3, ESV

Sister, here is another Love Nugget. Our Father had a special love for Jeremiah. He was young and had a willing heart. Although he constantly questioned the visions our Father gave him, he never doubted His love. Look up and feel the warmth of your Father's morning breeze falling gently across your face. His love is pure, clean, and full of joy. His love is like the sun rays gently feeding the morning lilies that bloom upon His plains. Sister, look how they dance in the wind. Do you see how they take in the sunshine and the rain? He knows no other way to express His sincere faithfulness to His servants but to love with a pure and innocent love. So leap into today with a love that is everlasting and one that will always be refreshing.

May 28

And Jesus answered them, "Have faith in God. Truly, I say to you, whoever says to this mountain, 'Be taken up and thrown into the sea,' and does not doubt in his heart, but believes that what he says will come to pass, it will be done for him." Mark 11:22-23, ESV

Sister, the Faith Nugget is the greatest of all nuggets because it is a gift and a fruit of the Holy Spirit. That is why it has so much power to declare, decree, and proclaim. This nugget gives you the power to speak things into existence that were not there. The key is that there should be no doubt or fear when faith is in operation. You must believe in your heart that all things are possible. So go forth and throw all your mountains into the sea.

May 29

Therefore I tell you, whatever you ask in prayer, believe that you have received it, and it will be yours. Mark 11:24, ESV

Sister, prayer is an important tool for the believer. Prayer, faith, and fasting bring things from the spiritual realm into the physical realm. Prayer is powerful because it can move through air, wood, soil, concrete, metal, water, and fire. There is no boundary prayer cannot cross.

May 30

For nothing will be impossible with God. Luke 1:37, ESV

Sister, when all else fails, try our Father. All things are possible with Him. So talk to Him and go into today with confidence and faith. Your Father has answered your prayers and moved all your problems from your mind and your living space.

May 31

For we walk by faith, not by sight. 2 Corinthians 5:7, ESV

Sister, how are you walking? If you are walking by sight, then your eyes are closed, and you will soon stumble and fall. Start walking by faith. Just believe and see what will happen. Without faith, it is impossible to please our God. So go faithfully into today seeing the things you desire in your mind first, and your Father will bring it to you right where you are. That is what we call walking by faith and believing that the things we ask for will appear before our eyes. As you walk, be patient. Your Father may not come when you want Him, but He will always be there on time. He is an on-time God.

JUNE

The Peony Symbolizes:
romance, a happy marriage, compassion, riches, prosperity, and honor

June 1

For your Maker is your husband, the Lord of hosts is his name; and the Holy One of Israel is your Redeemer, the God of the whole earth he is called. Isaiah 54:5, ESV

Daughter, I will be everything you need me to be. Whether you are alone, have a husband, or he no longer exists, I will provide food, shelter, and comfort in times of unrest. I am your Lord, your God, your Redeemer, and your heavenly Father. I created you and know the number of hairs in your head. I am here to protect you, to encourage you, and to carry you when you grow tired. I will keep your enemies from harming you and will restore everything you have lost. So go and walk in honor. I am the lover of your soul.

June 2

As we look not to the things that are seen but to the things that are unseen. For the things that are seen are transient, but the things that are unseen are eternal. 2 Corinthians 4:18, ESV

Sister, place your focus on things that are lasting and will not fade. Do not waste time on trivial things that are not going to help improve your future. Those things that you can see, touch, and feel with your hands will tarnish and go back to the dust. The things unseen will last forever. So greet today with a made-up mind to seek those things that bring happiness and joy.

June 3

For God gave us a spirit not of fear but of power and love and self-control. 2 Timothy 1:7, ESV

Sister, listen to this Self-Control Nugget. You must cast down all the imaginations and fears that enter your mind. They are not from our Father. He did not give us a spirit of fear or a spirit of imagination. He gave us a spirit of love, peace, and joy. These spirits will overcome the spirit of fear. The spirit of fear creates doubt, confusion, and unrest in your mind and soul. Our Father does not want us to be afraid or let fearful thoughts control us. He gives us inner peace to control our thoughts. When the spirit of fear rises up in us, His Spirit of power, love, and self-control take command of our spirit and crush the movement and thoughts of fear. So go joyfully into today. Fear has been destroyed.

June 4

Let not your hearts be troubled. Believe in God; believe also in me.
John 14:1, ESV

Sister, do not allow grief to conquer your heart and mind. Our Father is a powerful God and He will comfort you in your hour of loneliness. Has He not said to cast all your burdens upon Him and that He is strong enough to carry them all? Has He not been there for you through all your struggles and the trials that have confronted you? If you believe those words to be true, you must trust Him to know what is right for you. He will never leave you alone or lead you astray. He cares for you. So get up and have faith in your Father. Our Father knows best. He would never bring us this far to leave us.

June 5

But I discipline my body and keep it under control, lest after preaching to others I myself should be disqualified. 1 Corinthians 9:27, ESV

Sister, how can you tell someone how to deal with a problem when you are guilty of the same thing? What virtue is in it? You must learn to control your own body before you can give instructions to others and their bodies. Even Apostle Paul knew such a practice of leading and teaching others contrary to what our Father has taught would end his ministry. Such methods are will be contrary to the profession of which you have been called to perform in the physical world. There are people who emulate, model, and follow in your footsteps. When you show one good side and hide the bad side, it is no more than an apple that is pretty on the outside, but rotten to the core. Go quickly and make amends with your Father.

June 6

Be sober-minded; be watchful. Your adversary the devil prowls around like a roaring lion, seeking someone to devour. 1 Peter 5:8, ESV

It is a marvelous sight to see you move about in your circle of friends. You are doing good, spreading truth, and taking in the world. But, be careful; everyone is not happy for your blessings. There are those who have a jealous spirit and want harm to come to you. They will place stumbling blocks in your path to slow your progress. They will even devise ways to cause you to trip and fall. They are sly and manipulative, like the devil who is like a lion seeking whom he can destroy. Enter this day gentle as a lamb, but wise as an owl. Walk proud and keep your eye on the prize. Wait for your Father to reveal the right time, and then beat them at their own game.

June 7

Love is patient and kind; love does not envy or boast; it is not arrogant or rude. It does not insist on its own way; it is not irritable or resentful.
1 Corinthians 13:4-5, ESV

Daughter, do not love the world or the things that are only temporal. Love for the sake of loving, which will bring you joy in times of sorrow. It will be peace and kindness when there is no happiness in the world. This kind of love comes from me. I have given it to the world, but they have forsaken it, and their hatred for each other grows daily. Many will say they love you, but if their love is not patient or kind, and it is rude and conceited, love them from a distance. Go into today with my blessings, loving as I have taught you to love.

June 8

Set a guard, O LORD, over my mouth; keep watch over the door of my lips! Psalm 141:3, ESV

Father, I know there are times when I speak before I think. Then there are times when my tongue says things I do not want to say. I know it is wrong, because afterwards, my spirit feels sad and disturbed. But sometimes I am placed in situations where I must speak or forever hold my peace. It is during these times when trouble gets in my way and I just have to say something to release the pressure. Father, place your hand over my mouth and shut my lips tight when I am about to say things that cannot be placed back in my mouth. Just cover me as I go forward and move temptation out of my path. I know that I am still a work in progress and that you will continue to keep a watch over me.

June 9

You did not choose me, but I chose you and appointed you that you should go and bear fruit and that your fruit should abide, so that whatever you ask the Father in my name, he may give it to you.
John 15:16, ESV

Daughter, when you were in your mother's womb, I chose you as a faithful follower and gave you an anointing and an appointment. You were set aside from other daughters because of your strength, wisdom, and understanding. These attributes will bear the fruit of love, joy, peace, and meekness, and they will remain with you as long as you live. Everything that the world has in store for you is at your fingertips. I have declared and decreed that all you ask in my name is already there for you to receive. So go forward with my blessings. My truth marches on before you. It will blaze a path for you.

June 10

No one can serve two masters, for either he will hate the one and love the other, or he will be devoted to the one and despise the other. You cannot serve God and money. Matthew 6:24, ESV

Sister, there is no way that you can live a double life loving the things of this world today and forsaking the things of your Father tomorrow. A lifestyle like that will only anger Him. Your Father has taught you that when you are lukewarm like this, you will love one lifestyle and hate the other, and He will spew you out of his mouth. I pray that you will choose your Father and let go of the things that will cause you grief. In Philippians, He promised to "supply all your needs according to His riches in" heaven (4:19). Trust Him to lead you out.

June 11

But when he who had set me apart before I was born, and who called me by his grace, was pleased to reveal his Son to me, in order that I might preach him among the Gentiles, I did not immediately consult with anyone. Galatians 1:15-16, ESV

Sister, why are you seeking permission from others to do what your Father has decreed that you would do? Are His words not proof enough for your life? Can man give you more insight about your future than your own Father? Your Father knew you before you were born. He knew where you would live, your first love, and everything else about you. These people know you momentarily and they will soon forget, but your Father knows your comings and your goings. He will never leave or forget you. Whatever path you take, He will be there to lead and guide you. Go gracefully into this day walking in your Father's love.

June 12

And I heard the voice of the Lord saying, "Whom shall I send, and who will go for us?" Then I said, "Here I am! Send me." Isaiah 6:8, ESV

Father, I hear your voice calling me. I heard you years ago, but I was scared of what people would say. I came out of the world. The life I lived was not a righteous life. I drank strong drinks, took women's husbands, took food from their children, and now I am ashamed of the things I did. But once I got a taste of you, I did not want to go back to where I came from. I want to tell the world how good you are. I have no training and no voice to convince anyone that you sent me. But Father, I am ready to go wherever you send me. I am not scared because I know you will lead and teach me as I go.

June 13

In him we have obtained an inheritance, having been predestined according to the purpose of him who works all things according to the counsel of his will. Ephesians 1:11, ESV

You have already been set aside for an inheritance. I have already decreed and declared your future. The life you will live is spread before you like an open book. All you will need to do is make the pictures happen as I turn the pages. Your works have been recorded and they have not been found lacking in anything. Arise and go into this day. Your future is bright and glowing with happiness and success. The lives that are awaiting your coming will be blessed from just being in your presence.

June 14

If my people who are called by my name humble themselves, and pray and seek my face and turn from their wicked ways, then I will hear from heaven and will forgive their sin and heal their land.
2 Chronicles 7:14, ESV

I know there are many people who are afraid and have called upon me to lift the plague that I have allowed to come upon them. Several people who are called by my name (Christians) do not resemble me or think as I think. They have gone after other gods as they did in the days of my prophets. I will remove this veil soon, in just a little while, but they must feel my wrath. I am angry with their disobedient ways. But you and a remnant who keep my commandments will be spared. You shall live to see this plague leave the earth. You shall live to see a great number of people repent and return to their First Love. Then, and only then, will I receive them and heal their land.

June 15

Arise, shine, for your light has come, and the glory of the LORD has risen upon you. Isaiah 60:1, ESV

Come on and get up from your sleeping couch. There is much to be done. There is a blessing in store for you. It is time for you to come out of the shadows and start to shine. Your talents cannot be seen when they are hidden in the dark. The day has come for you to stop putting them on the back burner waiting for a convenient time to bring them out. Now is the time to show the world what your Father has provided for you. He is ready to use you for His praise and honor. Now, go forth and bask in the light of His glory. His light will make you known among people of all color, ages, titles, and positions. Be grateful and humble as you go.

June 16

*Surely goodness and mercy shall follow me all the days of my life, and I shall dwell in the house of the L*ORD *forever.* **Psalm 23:6, ESV**

Father, I just want to thank you for all you have done for me. You have been water when I was thirsty for a word of encouragement. You have been a shelter from the countless number of storms in my life. You have been a rock that I could hide under when my enemies were closing in on me. Father, you have been more than life to me. For without you, I would not have life. I have received your goodness, your grace, and your mercy ever since I decided to follow you. My life is forever in your capable and loving hands. I praise you and magnify your holy name. You are worthy to be praised. I shall live in your house forever, where there is love, peace, and happiness.

June 17

But they who wait for the LORD shall renew their strength; they shall mount up with wings like eagles; they shall run and not be weary; they shall walk and not faint. Isaiah 40:31, ESV

Lift up your wings and fly, my dear. Fly above the skies into the stars and around my world. You have been faithful because of your longsuffering and patience. Take the mighty wings of the eagle and fly over hills and mountains. You are being rewarded, because after all the glitter, bright lights, and fame that were offered, you refused them and kept walking. Even when you needed money, you waited to hear from me. Walk into my joy and my love. I will reward you openly for your obedience and sacrifice.

June 18

No weapon formed against you shall prosper, And every tongue which rises against you in judgment You shall condemn.
Isaiah 54:17, NKJV

Nothing can touch you when you are in my care. Many will try to pluck you out of my arms, but they will not have the power to move you. Ten thousand arrows may come at you, but they will all fall at your feet. No weapon can hurt you when you are in my care. Even the tongues that judged and spoke false words against you will speak no more. You have the authority to condemn, rebuke, and reprove them. While you are in my protective care, no weapon pointed toward you will succeed. So go in peace. I have destroyed all those weapons. You will have peace in the valley and on the mountaintop.

June 19

If any of you lacks wisdom, let him ask God, who gives generously to all without reproach, and it will be given him. James 1:5, ESV

The Wisdom Nugget is a gift that comes from your Father. It cannot be purchased, sold, or captured. You cannot receive it from an institution. Others cannot give it to you, and you are not born with it. If you or anyone among you seek wisdom, they must go to our Father and ask Him in open conversation or prayer. He will give it to them freely without disapproval. The only cost is taking time to understand His statutes. He will tell you that along with wisdom comes understanding. These nuggets complement each other. One will not be effective without the other.

June 20

Rejoice always, pray without ceasing, give thanks in all circumstances; for this is the will of God in Christ Jesus for you.
1 Thessalonians 5:16-18, ESV

Sister, there is no better life than knowing that the skills, talents, and gifts you have achieved are the result of the love and protection of your Father. His treasures are filled with rewards and blessings that are too many to count. Therefore, look up to praise Him and thank Him, no matter what your situation may be. If it were not for Him, where would you be? Always pray constantly, being careful not to ask for inappropriate things. So rejoice as you greet this day. This is your Father's will for your future. He cares about you and wants you to be happy and successful in all the things you endeavor to do in your life.

June 21

Iron sharpens iron, and one man sharpens another.
Proverbs 27:17, ESV

Never allow anyone to teach or train you whose skills and talents are less than your gifts. You are setting yourself up for shame and defeat when people who are weak in their teaching skills want to teach you. Treat them with respect and offer any assistance to accommodate them when asked. When you allow people who have less skills to teach and train you, it lessens and drains your skills. They get stronger while you get weaker. How can you advance further when you associate with people who don't know what you know? If you want more out of your profession, work with people who know more than you. When you get where they are or above them, go back and train those you left behind.

June 22

Keep your heart with all vigilance, for from it flow the springs of life.
Proverbs 4:23, ESV

Sister, your heart is the most important organ in your body. Not only does it serve as a reservoir to transport blood throughout your systems to sustain the physical body, but "out of the abundance of the heart the mouth speaks" (Matthew 12:34, NJKV). So guard the lips of your mouth for the living waters of life flow through it. Keep your heart pure and guard it with all carefulness. Do not allow it to be a place of corruption and evil intentions. The seeds of malice, hatred, lies, and misgivings are found in the heart. The day will come when you will be asked to present yourself before your Father to speak on the hidden treasures that lie within your heart.

June 23

Bring the full tithe into the storehouse, that there may be food in my house. And thereby put me to the test, says the LORD of hosts, if I will not open the windows of heaven for you and pour down for you a blessing until there is no more need. Malachi 3:10, ESV

Sister, come and let me tell you about the Wealth Nugget. Do you ever wonder why some people have an abundance of wealth spiritually and physically, while others just barely have enough to get by? Do you see some people driving two and three cars, while others have only one car and it stays at the mechanic all the time? How about the big houses and the weekend trips? Yes, I know you think this is extravagant, but these people put God to the test. They gave only 10% of their earnings to our Father's house and He kept His promise by pouring blessings on them that they did not have room to put them in. Tell the people to start tithing to get full blessings from our Father.

June 24

And if I have prophetic powers, and understand all mysteries and all knowledge, and if I have all faith, so as to remove mountains, but have not love, I am nothing. 1 Corinthians 13:2, ESV

Daughter, do not get caught up in the glamour of prophesying as other daughters have done and lost their calling. Do not even try to understand the mysteries that happen in the universe or try to receive all the knowledge found in books and men of old. You may have many of these qualities and can operate sufficiently in them, and your faith may be strong enough to speak to mountains and they may move. But, dear, if there is no love in your heart for others, then you are nothing. So love your enemies and do good to those who forsake you.

June 25

And without faith it is impossible to please him, for whoever would draw near to God must believe that he exists and that he rewards those who seek him. Hebrews 11:6, ESV

Come and listen to the greatest Faith Nugget of all. Many people think they may please our Father by doing great works in the church. There are some who think that by paying large sums of money, they can capture His heart. Then there are others who think it is in quoting scriptures from memory. They can do all these things and more. But, sister, if they do not have any faith, it is impossible to please our Father. So go about your work faithfully pleasing your Father today. The works you have shown are not dead. They are alive and well.

June 26

But let him ask in faith, with no doubting, for the one who doubts is like a wave of the sea that is driven and tossed by the wind.
James 1:6, ESV

Sister, if you want this promotion and recognition, believe that you already have it and it will be yours. Whenever you doubt yourself, you are like a water wave driven and tossed by the wind. It cancels everything out. Your Father has already shown you in the spiritual realm what will be yours in the physical realm. You have worked very hard for this event. Now start believing in yourself. Close your eyes, look in your mind, and see yourself walking toward your dream. If you cannot see it, then it is not time to be revealed. But if you can see it, in a little while, you will see it be manifested in the physical realm. So go ahead and shout, "Hallelujah!" Sing praises to your Father.

June 27

For with the heart one believes and is justified, and with the mouth one confesses and is saved. Romans 10:10, ESV

The Salvation Nugget is a powerful nugget because it was created when Jesus Christ died on the cross. Apostle Paul, who persecuted the early Christians, received this nugget on the Damascus Road and began to offer it to others by asking them to believe with their hearts, confess with their mouths, and they will be saved. So you see, no one was saved before Christ came into the world. They were justified by the Faith Nugget. The Salvation Nugget, like all the other nuggets, is free and does not cost anything. Sister, go and get your salvation.

June 28

Therefore do not throw away your confidence, which has a great reward. **Hebrews 10:35, ESV**

Do not lose confidence in yourself. It is a gateway through which you will gain insight into your future. Your life was not given to you to throw away. There was a great amount of precious blood shed so that you can be the person your Father has ordained you to become. So get up and shake off this cloud of gloom. You were created for greatness. Do not let the enemy steal your joy. Put on the whole armor of faith, hope, and love. You shall overcome this period of unbelief and distrust in your life. So walk with your head held high. Your Father is getting ready to reward you for your confidence and inner strength. Do not disappoint Him. But most of all, do not disappoint yourself.

June 29

Blessed is the man who trusts in the LORD, whose trust is the LORD. He is like a tree planted by water, that sends out its roots by the stream, and does not fear when heat comes, for its leaves remain green, and is not anxious in the year of drought, for it does not cease to bear fruit.
Jeremiah 17:7-8, ESV

Do not be fearful of things that cause you to run and find refuge. Trust our Father. He will protect you. He will lead you to green pastures where there is food and water. You will always find a shelter from the storm and the heat. When others around you are falling and feeling the pains of sickness, you will stand and remain healthy. Your children will grow up strong and prosperous. Prosperity and blessings shall follow you, your children, and your children's children, as long as the east remains separated from the west.

June 30

Do all things without grumbling or disputing.
Philippians 2:14, ESV

Do not be so quick to complain when you are asked to perform a duty for an elderly or a younger person. Neither question them when they tell you to do good works in the name of your Father. It is a good thing to help those who cannot help themselves. Your Father sees everything you do and is keeping record of all the good and wrong deeds done. Your chances of pleasing Him and receiving a reward for obedience is better when you help those who need your service, than grumbling and complaining. So go forth into today with a caring spirit of love and a desire to help those in need. Your Father will reward you for serving others, which in turn serves Him.

JULY

The Day Lily Symbolizes:
the sacrifice a mother has for her child, the love a child has for her mother, devotion, and forgetting painful memories of sorrow and

July 1

Let each of you look not only to his own interests, but also to the interests of others. Philippians 2:4, ESV

Sister, you have been faithful, courageous, and steadfast over the years in your desire to reach out and help people. You never showed partiality or favoritism toward any person. There is a standard you always adhere to and hold high as you carry out your tasks in greeting and talking to people. Your Father is watching you and is pleased with your devotion and the love you have for the least of these. So go joyfully into today. Your Father has a blessing for you.

July 2

We who are strong have an obligation to bear with the failings of the weak, and not to please ourselves. Romans 15:1, ESV

You have great strength and self-control. The circles you move in have much respect and high regards for you. They admire the way you are always genuinely supporting, defending, and encouraging the weak to be strong in spite of oppositions and struggles. Go into today with praise in helping those who need care and support. Great is your reward in heaven.

July 3

Remember not the former things, nor consider the things of old. Behold, I am doing a new thing; now it springs forth, do you not perceive it? I will make a way in the wilderness and rivers in the desert.
Isaiah 43:18-19, ESV

Child, why are you pondering over the past? There is nothing you can do there. The past is gone forever. It is like grass that is withered from the heat of the sun. Release it now and forget about the things that caused you pain and grief. All those old things are like water that has passed under the bridge; it will not come back again. I am getting ready to do a new thing in your life. A bright future is in store for you. The people who questioned your capabilities and integrity will have to bow to you as the brothers of Joseph bowed to him. Opportunities will come and blessings will flow from all directions. So rejoice and greet this day with a smile on your face.

July 4

Not that I have already obtained this or am already perfect, but I press on to make it my own, because Christ Jesus has made me his own.
Philippians 3:12, ESV

You are made from the special dust that your Father has sprinkled with love, wisdom, and understanding. You already see around the corner and have claimed what is already yours. You have determination ingrained within you and know what it means to fight the good fight. There are no boundaries you will not cross because your Father will be there helping you over mountains and holding your hand. So greet this day with joy. You know who is in you, who owns you, and who speaks for you. Goodness and blessings shall follow you.

July 5

Some trust in chariots and some in horses, but we trust in the name of the LORD our God. Psalm 20:7, ESV

Why are you still believing in the strength of material things and the lies told by ambitious men who seek personal gain? Have any of them proven to be true? If you cannot find one trace of evidence that they are right, then why trust them? Material things will fade away. They will rust and decay. Men will always chase them, looking for a quick rise to fame and power. Place your focus on things that are lasting and eternal, and that is our Father. His name is known throughout the universe. He has proven His power and trust time after time. So run into today with a steadfast trust in your Father. You can stretch your hand to Him and find truth and help.

July 6

I press on toward the goal for the prize of the upward call of God in Christ Jesus. Philippians 3:14, ESV

Sister, you cannot stop now. Your Father has brought you too far for you to sit down on Him and all the plans you have made. Get up and get back in this race. The reward is too great to just close your eyes and throw it away. There are many more miles to run before you see the finish line. Keep on moving in spite of all the runners you will see fallen by the side of the road. There is nothing you can do for them, except to pray for them. Run when adverse talk and the clutter of noise block your ears. Keep your eyes on the prize and your Father will lead you over the victory line. So put on your running shoes and take back your place in this race. This is only one race in the course of many more races you will run. Your Father will always run beside you.

July 7

Not that we are sufficient in ourselves to claim anything as coming from us, but our sufficiency is from God. 2 Corinthians 3:5, ESV

No, not for one moment should you think that you, yourself, have power, strength, courage, and wisdom to complete these tasks. You can never take credit for them because these gifts are rewards and blessings that come from your Father. He has given these gifts unselfishly to anyone who follows His precepts and trusts completely in Him. We can do nothing without Him. We are so fortunate to be claimed by Him as His beloved daughters. That is why we must always trust Him and place all of our wants and needs before Him in prayer.

July 8

Yet you do not know what tomorrow will bring. What is your life? For you are a mist that appears for a little time and then vanishes. Instead you ought to say, "If the Lord wills, we will live and do this or that."
James 4:14-15, ESV

Sister, never put off tomorrow what you can do today. If you have plans and you are pondering over when to start them, do it now. Who knows what tomorrow will bring or if we may even be alive? While we can feel life moving through our bodies, we should work while it is day. It is our Father who controls the time, the days, and the breath we breathe. So move into this day making preparations to do what you have placed on the back burner for years. Your Father is ready to show you the way. He will never place you in a position and leave you there to carry it through all alone. He is your provider and your supplier. Put all your trust in Him and He will walk with you as you start this task.

July 9

Joseph called the name of the firstborn Manasseh. "For," he said, "God has made me forget all my hardship and all my father's house."
Genesis 41:51, ESV

Daughter, few people have lived through rejection and loneliness as my son Joseph. Remember, his brothers sold him to the Ishmaelites for twenty pieces of silver. They took him to Egypt where he was imprisoned and was finally blessed beyond measure. If Joseph forgot his past and was blessed too, will I not do the same for you? Place all these memories of pain, hurt, and disappointments upon my shoulder and I will carry them for you. "For my yoke *is* easy, and my burden is light" (Matthew 11:30, KJV). I know where there is a place of forgetfulness. I will throw them there and they will never resurface again. So go forward with your life and expect the best. I am always with you.

July 10

__Your word is a lamp to my feet and a light to my path.__
__Psalm 119:105, ESV__

Father, every time I hear or speak your words, my body catches on fire. The energy from your fire lights the lamp that brightens the path where I walk. I am so honored and grateful to be called your daughter. You give me a reason to shine when darkness and gloom cover my paths. You put a burst of joy and laughter on my lips. I have to continually praise your name day and night. Father, you cause the fire in my heart to blaze with a vibrant flame that warms my entire body with love and peace. You are the shining light upon a hill, and I will forever look up to you. You light up my life.

July 11

Can a woman forget her nursing child, that she should have no compassion on the son of her womb? Even these may forget, yet I will not forget you. Isaiah 49:15, ESV

My sweet child, how can I ever forget you? You are always in my thoughts. I formed you and gave you a place of warmth and safety. I laid you down to sleep last night, and this morning, I whispered in your ear to awaken you from your sleeping couch. Then, I placed food on your table. I knew you when you were in your mother's womb. I nursed you from your youth to the woman you have become today. No mother can love her child like I love you. Many mothers gave birth and have left or forsaken their children. I promise to never leave or ever forget you.

July 12

The king is not saved by his great army; a warrior is not delivered by his great strength. Psalm 33:16, ESV

You may have many people who are following you now, but the time will come when they will question your integrity and beliefs. They will come against you and ask you to validate your authority and position. Remember that it is not the leader who saves the people or a movement, nor is it the warrior who shows strength and endurance that saves the multitude. It is the mercy and grace showered upon them by your Father because of the cause in which they fight. Never think that you are the source of the power or the victory that is the result of a war. There will come a time when you will have to stand on your own merits. Make sure they are for the right cause and that your Father is the one who is in control.

July 13

I have confidence in the Lord that you will take no other view, and the one who is troubling you will bear the penalty, whoever he is.
Galatians 5:10, ESV

There were followers of Jesus Christ in Galatia who were harassed by false teachers trying to change their mind about the sound teachings of Apostle Paul. Paul tells them not to worry because God will erase the words of the false teachers from their minds and seal their minds with the words of Jesus Christ. Sister, if your Father can do this over 2000 years ago, will He not do the same for you? You will always have people in all professions that will try to disrupt your progress. Leave them alone. When the words have the blessings of your Father, they will stand. Now, go in peace and continue to do good works.

July 14

Likewise the Spirit helps us in our weakness. For we do not know what to pray for as we ought, but the Spirit himself intercedes for us with groanings too deep for words. Romans 8:26, ESV

There are times when we pray and the words just do not pour out like they used to. We just sit there swaying back and forth. Then the Holy Spirit that is within us takes over. He starts to groan and moan for us and speak on our behalf. It is not important to us what He says to our Father. We know that whatever it is, it helps us. He knows our needs and carries those needs to our Father for us. Our Father responds by calming us and allowing us to speak to Him. We must remember to give Him praise and bless Him for His faithfulness. So greet this day with the faithfulness of your Father. He has made you stronger and greater than your weaknesses to face another day.

July 15

The LORD will keep you from all evil; he will keep your life. The LORD will keep your going out and your coming in from this time forth and forevermore. Psalm 121:7-8, ESV

Daughter, I am your keeper. I will keep harm and danger from entering your home. I will keep your enemies from overcoming you and will make them your footstool. I will keep you from falling and will carry you when you grow tired and weak. I am the lover and keeper of your soul. I am here to walk with you and to talk with you. I am here to be your Father and your friend when all have left and gone their separate ways. I see you when you go out and when you come in. Go freely into this day knowing that in all you do and in all you say, your keeper is always watching you.

July 16

As in water face reflects face, so the heart of man reflects the man.
Proverbs 27:19, ESV

Sister, be careful about letting just any man enter the doors of your heart. Verify that he is real in all he says and all he does. You are very high temperate and do not like to be taken advantage of nor taken for granted. Try his spirit by the Spirit of your Father to see if he has the spirit of Boaz. If he does, then treat him with kindness. This is the man our Father has sent to treat you as a princess. If his spirit vexes you in any way, then turn aside from him and let him go on his way; this is not the man your Father wants you to be a part of. So go joyfully into this day and wait for your Father to send you a good man – one who loves Him and walks in His precepts.

July 17

Through him then let us continually offer up a sacrifice of praise to God, that is, the fruit of lips that acknowledge his name.
Hebrews 13:15, ESV

Father, you are my everything. I worship you and give you the highest praise. I magnify your holy name and give you honor and glory. You are my guiding light and you're always there when I desperately need you. You were there for me in sickness and in health. You kept my home and family safe. You are worthy to be praised. There is no other Father like you. There is safety in your arms, warmth in your touch, love in your heart, and healing in your name. I will forever be grateful that I am your daughter.

July 18

I cried aloud to the LORD, and he answered me from his holy hill. Selah. I lay down and slept; I woke again, for the LORD sustained me.
Psalm 3:4-5, ESV

Have no fear, my child. I hear your fervid cry. Your cry reaches all the way to Zion. I will answer you out of my holy hill as I answered my servant David. Do you remember when David cried to me because his enemies chased him day and night? He had no rest. I laid him down to sleep and awakened him in the morning. You are worn and tired. I will also lay you down to a peaceful sleep and watch over you until the morning comes. Then, I will wake you again, giving you a breath of fresh air and cool spiritual water to continue your journey. So arise and go into this day with strength, comfort, and blessings following you. I will always be a heartbeat away from you, keeping you safe and hearing your call.

July 19

"Blessed is she who has believed that the Lord would fulfill his promises to her!" Luke 1:45, NIV

Daughter, what a spirit of strength and confidence you have shown and delivered throughout your life. There have been many complications and struggles that you have overcome. Your faith is rooted and grounded in my precepts and my statutes. You have climbed many mountains and conquered many tasks. You were born for such a time as this, to show my courage, patience, and perseverance. There is no doubt that you trust and believe in me. Child, your days of pain, sickness, and unfulfillment are over. I will shower you with all the blessings I have promised you. So leap into today. Your dreams are at hand.

July 20

She is clothed with strength and dignity; she can laugh at the days to come. Proverbs 31:25, NIV

Daughter, you wear your struggles with great strength and grace. No one would ever know the things you have denied yourself, the pain you have endured, and yet, you still walk in dignity and demand respect. Your very nature is a daughter who is a warrior and a survivor. I have seen the enemy run when he sees you coming. He knows your strength and has heard your laughter about what others fear and shudder in defeat. Go forward into this day with no fear of the enemy or danger awaiting you. I am your Father, and I will cover you as you go. I will also increase your faith and your strength.

July 21

Woe to him who says to wood, 'Come to life!' Or to lifeless stone, 'Wake up!' Can it give guidance? It is covered with gold and silver; there is no breath in it. Habakkuk 2:19, NIV

Be careful not to put all your confidence and faith in people who promise you the stars and end up giving you an imitation of the real thing. They will try to convince you that life is found in trinkets and gemstones. These people are found in high places in the religious, governmental, educational, and other professional fields. They will dangle the golden ring before you, and when you have done everything to receive it, the ring vanishes. Your Father did not teach you to be fooled by these trinkets. These things cannot give you wisdom or understanding. They do not even have life to speak to you. So as you meet this day, keep your eye on the prize which lives in your Father.

July 22

*And the L*ORD *answered me, and said, Write the vision, and make it plain upon tables, that he may run that readeth it.* Habakkuk 2:2, KJV

Sister, never speak the visions your Father has given you aloud or into the atmosphere. There are always itching ears waiting to take your vision and claim it as their own. When God gives you a vision, write it down and make it plain so that whoever reads it will know that it came from your Father. They will read it and see that it is impossible for them to imitate. When they see God's hand in the making of your vision, they will quickly run away in fear. So approach this day with joy in your heart. For in a little while, your Father will speak to you and He will bring your vision into the physical world.

July 23

O Lord, you have searched me and known me! You know when I sit down and when I rise up; you discern my thoughts from afar.
Psalm 139:1-2, ESV

Father, you know me so well. You knew my thoughts before I formed them in my mind. You knew the words I would say while they were forming on my lips. Father, you knew who I would spend my life with and the number of children I would birth. You know everything about me. There is no place I can go where you are not there. Father, thank you for my comings and my goings. Thank you for keeping me safe from my enemies and allowing my days to grow longer upon this earth. I am grateful that you are my Father. I will cast all my cares upon you because I know that you love my soul.

July 24

And let the peace that comes from Christ rule in your hearts. For as members of one body you are called to live in peace. And always be thankful. **Colossians 3:15, NLT**

Thank you, Father, for the spirit of peace that rules my mind, body, and soul. I am at peace with the world and have no hatred in my heart for anyone. I realize that if I am going to be one with you, your Son, and your Spirit, I must show that I am peaceful and become a keeper of peace. Everywhere I go, I will move in circles where there is respect and love for your word. I will speak words of joy, love, and kindness that will bring happiness to the minds and hearts of those who hear my voice. I am an ambassador of peace and I will spread goodness, kindness, and happiness everywhere.

July 25

'For I will heal you. I will heal you where you have been hurt,' says the Lord, 'because they have said that you are not wanted. They have said, "It is Zion. No one cares for her."' Jeremiah 30:17, NLV

Have no more fear for your future, my child. I am here to heal your body and anything else that causes you pain. Just as I removed the nations in Israel's path and restored them to where they once were, I will also remove those who have caused you grief. You are the daughter of a King. They will honor and respect you for who you are. So walk with grace and beauty into this day. I will restore your health in your body and in all that you do. I am your Father. I will always love you and provide for your care and protection.

July 26

When she speaks, her words are wise, and she gives instructions with kindness. Proverbs 31:26, NLT

Daughter, when you speak, the sounds of wisdom and love flow from your heart. You are genuine and filled with all the fruit of my Spirit. Your spirit is so gentle and kind. It ministers to those who are poor in their spirit and it gives strength to the ones who are weak in their minds. Yes, you are my special daughter. You have a heart to cure the ills of the world. There are times when you are oppressed, but you leave your troubles behind to give words of comfort and joy to the afflicted, the lost, and to those in distress. Your gifts of love, patience, and long-suffering light up the faces of those who are touched by your kindness. Go into this day with hope, faith, and love walking joyfully beside you.

July 27

"How long will you go here and there, O daughter without faith? For the Lord has made a new thing on the earth: A woman will keep a man safe." Jeremiah 31:22, NLV

Stop looking for favor and peace from men who do not know me. Daughter, start preparing for your future. The time is coming when my daughters shall sit in places of authority and shall rule my people with love and humility. Your faith is strong and there is determination and ambition in the way you talk and the way you walk. You have the makings of a warrior. Gather your quiver and fill it with weapons of wisdom, understanding, and love. You have prepared and set the table for a long time. You have even served the food. Now it is time, my princess, for you to have a seat at the table that I shall prepare for my daughters. Get up and move quickly because judgment is at hand and my daughters will reap where they have not sown.

July 28

You are great in wisdom and powerful in Your works. Your eyes are open to all the ways of men. You pay every one for what he does and for the fruit of what he does. Jeremiah 32:19, NLV

Come, listen to this Prayer Nugget. Prophet Jeremiah is praying to our Father for the lives of the people. The people were disobedient, and our Father is getting ready to turn them over to the Babylonians. Sister, when trouble comes, we need to rise up and pray. Do you see how Jeremiah begins his prayer? He recognizes the greatness in wisdom and the powerful works of our Father. Then he praises our Father for His all-seeing eyes and acknowledges, whether good or bad, the Lord rewards all for their deeds. Sister, we need to pray for mercy and healing for our nation.

July 29

__But he knows the way that I take; when he has tried me, I shall come out as gold. Job 23:10, ESV__

Sister, just as our Father knew Job's heart was clean, He also knows our hearts. Our Father has to test us as well. Just because some people are tried with sickness or pain, doesn't mean that they have committed any wrongs. So as you are tested, pass your test. If you are tried by fire, you will come forth as pure as gold.

July 30

For you know that the testing of your faith produces steadfastness.
James 1:3, ESV

When someone is doubtful of what they believe, they are like a ship upon the sea, driven by the wind, moving from side to side. That is why our Father tests our faith so we will not waver from knowing and speaking the truth. You will be better when your faith is strong.

July 31

Peace I leave with you; my peace I give you. I do not give to you as the world gives. Do not let your hearts be troubled and do not be afraid.
John 14.27, NIV

My precious child, the peace I leave with you is real peace that is lasting and not like the peace that is promised by man that never appears. I am there to give you inner peace that surpasses all understanding. I am here to calm your heart so that you will be done with the troubles that cause you grief and sorrow. My peace will bring you joy in the midst of your storms and trials. My peace brings happiness where there is sadness. So enter this day with my everlasting peace.

AUGUST

The Cosmos Flower Symbolizes:
tranquility, peace, harmony, and love

August 1

Long life is in her right hand; in her left hand are riches and honor.
Proverbs 3:16, ESV

Daughter, you are blessed beyond measure. I have given you a gift from the waters from which flows all life-giving substances. This source flows with rich minerals that prolong health and give strength to your body. You are fortunate to receive the blessings that are showered upon you. Because you are my special daughter, you hold within your hand the treasures of wealth and prosperity. Many people shall respect and honor your wisdom because of your long life. Go gracefully into this day receiving the riches and long life that awaits you.

August 2

For the sake of Christ, then, I am content with weaknesses, insults, hardships, persecutions, and calamities. For when I am weak, then I am strong. 2 Corinthians 12:10, ESV

Father, there are no aches or pains in my body. I woke up this morning with peace and love in my heart. You have carried me through all my troubles, opened and closed doors, as well as protected me from my enemies. I have learned that through all of my weaknesses you have made me strong. I am now able to follow the path that you have created for me with confidence and faith that if I fall, you will be there to pick me up. Thank you, Father, for loving me.

August 3

Even to your old age I am he, and to gray hairs I will carry you. I have made, and I will bear; I will carry and will save. Isaiah 46:4, ESV

Daughter, whether you have reached the years where the embers and passion in your life are dying out or at a youthful age where the flames are glowing strong, I will always be with you. I will bear your burdens when you grow tired. I will make your enemies your footstool. I will pick you up and carry you when you grow weak, and I will save you from the snares of the wicked. Daughter, I created you. I know the number of hairs on your head and your final day upon this earth. I will cover you as you sleep, as you walk, and as you work. You will always be my beloved princess. How can I ever leave or forsake you? Arise and walk into this day with grace and beauty.

August 4

These things speak and exhort and reprove with all authority. Let no one disregard you. Titus 2:15, NASB

No one can usurp your authority or steal the integrity, strength, and courage that have been bestowed upon you. Your Father looked within your heart and saw a special love and a faithful desire to reach out to others and make them feel appreciated and loved. He saw the loyalty you show to those in your care and how you have neglected yourself so that they may feel the warmth of peace and happiness. Your sacrifices have not gone unnoticed. As you enter into this day and throughout the coming days, there will be grace and mercy that will follow you all the days of your life.

August 5

Reject a factious man after a first and second warning.
Titus 3:10, NASB

Sister, allow no man to talk down to you. Your character is one of honor and faithfulness. You are called to service and duty for the Lord. Do not engage in foolish conversation with him because he is determined to embarrass you and as he would say, "Put you in your place." Just smile, be silent, and ignore him, unless your Father gives you a word of wisdom to leave with him. Proverbs 21:9 says, "It is better to live in a corner of the housetop than in a house shared with a quarrelsome wife" (ESV). So choose well when you think your Boaz has chosen you. Ask your Father for guidance.

August 6

My soul longs, yes, faints for the courts of the LORD; my heart and flesh sing for joy to the living God. Psalm 84:2, ESV

Father, when I think about the love you have for me, my heart lights up with joy. I know so well why King David sang this song. I know the bliss and happiness he felt to know that your love is real, true, and endless. Father, I am feeling the same way today. You have guided me in my career choices and have paved all my paths so I would not stumble or fall. I do not know where I would be without you loving me and caring for me. Father, you gave me a glorious morning. I feel great about this day and what is in store for me. I have no worries because you do not want me to fear anyone, or even allow the thought of defeat or failure to enter my mind. Father, you are my shining star.

August 7

We love because he first loved us. 1 John 4:19, ESV

No matter what other people say to us or how they treat us, we must still show that we have love in our hearts for them. When we show any other emotion except love, it gives the world the impression that we are not our Father's daughters. Our Father has told us that the people in this world will try to discourage, persecute, and accuse us of wrongdoings. But in spite of these attacks, we must continue to love them because our Father first loved us. Sister, we cannot even begin to show unconditional love unless the love of our Father is in us. So go lovingly into this day, forgiving those who speak evil of you or ridicule you. Remember that the world also spoke evil of His Son and even killed Him, but He arose from the grave victoriously.

August 8

Let love be genuine. Abhor what is evil; hold fast to what is good.
Romans 12:9, ESV

Sister, when you say, "I love you," whether in intimacy or generally speaking to the public, let it be real and impartial. Avoid all appearances of evil, for it will place shadows upon your loyalty and devotion to our Father. So many people are starving for love and they need to know that the love shown to them is solid like a rock. When that rock is Jesus, you can show love for all people. You don't have to validate or give a reason why you love them; you just do it. All you need to do is speak and the sound of your voice will show that you have been in the presence of the Almighty. So go into this day with a made-up mind for doing good. All the people who hear your voice will see love in your heart and will reward you with goodness and blessings.

August 9

Peter said to him, "Even if I must die with you, I will not deny you!" And all the disciples said the same. Matthew 26:35, ESV

Be careful when you make promises to people, not knowing whether or not you will be able to keep them. Do you remember what happened to Peter? He promised to never deny Jesus, but when the pressure was more than he could endure, he left and cried because he did not have the courage to defend Him. Even His disciples did the same thing when He faced death. Make sure your loyalty for a cause is real and that you will be able to suffer the consequences when your faith is tested. If you have to walk away or back down as Peter did, your character and integrity will suffer greatly. So go into this day seeking the advice and counsel of your Father who opens the door to tomorrow. He will not withhold from you anything you ask of Him.

August 10

Be watchful, stand firm in the faith, act like men, be strong. Let all that you do be done in love. 1 Corinthians 16:13-14, ESV

Sister, here is a nugget called a Strong Nugget. Although it is different, it is a powerful nugget because Paul is asking us to mount up as men in our minds and be strong as they are when going into battle. He knows that when men go to war, they will slay, destroy, and imprison the enemy and render him helpless. Sister, we are fighting a war every day and we must be prepared to wage war against the world. But as we fight today, let us go forward with our greatest weapon which is love. Godly love crushes and destroys the heart of the enemy because she does not recognize this emotion. So continue to love your enemies and she will become one of your trusted your friends.

August 11

If the anger of the ruler rises against you, do not leave your place, for calmness will lay great offenses to rest. **Ecclesiastes 10:4, ESV**

Be calm when people in authority, such as a supervisor, director, administrator, or any person over you, questions your integrity. Stand firm and hold your peace. Your Father will place words in your mouth that will resolve the issue. When you do speak, the words will come forth like a waterfall crashing against the rocks, moving structures, and changing boundaries in its path. They will know that your purpose and plan have been ordained by your Father. After the show of discipline and physical strength in your composure, they will not confront you again. So greet this day with a triumphant walk and a beat of confidence in your heart.

August 12

When Abram was ninety-nine years old the LORD appeared to Abram and said to him, "I am God Almighty; walk before me, and be blameless." Genesis 17:1, ESV

Yes, dear, it is your Father. I have called you to do this work. I have watched you from afar and have seen your loneliness and desire to help others. I am not concerned about your age. Look at the age of Abraham when I set him apart to be the Father of the Hebrew Nation. Never count me out and I will not give up on you. I know your strength and your willpower. You still have the same confidence and courage you possessed when you were young. You will perform those same duties as before, but only better because you have aged with much wisdom and understanding. Go forth into today walking before me in faithfulness and courage. I will cover you on all sides as you go forth.

August 13

For everything there is a season, and a time for every matter under heaven. **Ecclesiastes 3:1, ESV**

Do not be in such a hurry to perform this task during this unpredictable time in the nation. Check to see if it is even needed and if it has been tried before. It may very well work and sometimes it will, but is this the right time to pursue a venture of this nature? I know there is a saying, "You should never put off tomorrow what you could do today." That is a true saying. Look around and see what the mental, physical, and emotional pain will cost. Then, add up the cost to see if it is worth the time. Your Father will guide and cover you, but there may not be the same protection for others. So go into today weighing all your options before beginning this task.

August 14

Do you not know that in a race all the runners run, but only one gets the prize? Run in such a way as to get the prize.
1 Corinthians 9:24, NIV

Sister, life is full of Self-Disciplined Nuggets. Here is one that is a spiritual asset for every person who is running in the race of life. This race should not be taken for granted. You should not expect anyone to run it for you. We were born in a race when we first opened our eyes in this world. Each lap ran gets us closer to the finish line. Your Father will be on the path to help you as you run to give you strength and courage as you need them. We all have goals and promises made to ourselves and to others. These goals are determined by how hard and fast we will run to receive those things we have dreamed of obtaining. So as you approach this day, run strong, run long, and run with integrity. The prize may be years away, but run to win it. The ones who survives the run will receive their rewards.

August 15

For still the vision awaits its appointed time; it hastens to the end—it will not lie. If it seems slow, wait for it; it will surely come; it will not delay. **Habakkuk 2:3, ESV**

The Vision Nugget does not come to everyone. You are blessed that your Father has given you this vision. He gives it freely to those who follow His teachings and precepts. He looked into your future and has given this vision to you to let you get a glimpse of what is about to take place in your life. The vision does not happen instantly but it will appear and will reveal the same things that were seen in the spirit realm. It will linger for a while until the time is ripe for its entry into the physical realm. Do not be anxious for its appearance. Wait for it and it will reveal itself. So walk patiently into this day knowing that your Father knows your future and will protect and cover you as you walk.

August 16

Arise, for it is your task, and we are with you; be strong and do it.
Ezra 10:4, ESV

Sister, you think you have a hard choice to make that will affect others? Well, what about Ezra, the priest of Israel, who had to tell all the men of Israel they have to leave their wives and children and return to the God of their fathers? These men had married women from heathen nations that served idol gods. Ezra told the men that it was their job to choose God or their families. As you can see, you are not the only one to make a tough choice. Just as Ezra said to his people, do you hear a similar voice telling you to, "Get up. You must make this choice. We are with you?" You have to approach this problem head-on. Be strong; your Father is with you. There is nothing that is too hard for Him. Seek His advice and do what must be done.

August 17

But for this purpose I have raised you up, to show you my power, so that my name may be proclaimed in all the earth. Exodus 9:16, ESV

Do not be anxious or afraid of someone who is overbearing and want to be a god over you. Sometimes God raises these people up just for His purpose and when the right time comes, He uses them to make an example of them to show His power and His glory. God told Moses exactly what to tell Pharaoh. He destroyed Pharaoh in the Red Sea. So be patient. In just a little while, the Pharaoh(s) of your life will be destroyed, and God's name will be worshipped and praised in all the earth.

August 18

People with integrity walk safely, but those who follow crooked paths will be exposed. Proverbs 10:9, NLT

There are a number of paths walked by different people. Some walk crooked paths whose end is failure and destruction. The path you have chosen to walk is admirable. Your walk is one of humility, honor, and honesty. Many people will see your walk and will want to be just like you. Therefore, walk with strength, courage, and moral conviction. Your walk speaks volume of who you are, what you stand for, and where you are going. The path you blazed will be used for the safety of young feet coming after you, seeking truth and justice. Your Father is proud of your devotion and your eagerness to reach out and help others. So go forth walking in grace, faith, and truth.

August 19

The LORD of hosts has sworn: "As I have planned, so shall it be, and as I have purposed, so shall it stand." Isaiah 14:24, ESV

Why are you distressed about this trial? It is only a test. All tests are not final for all people, especially when you know that your Father has planned all things in your favor. If He has seen you through many tests before, some more dreadful than this one, then why would you think He will not see you through this test? God has planned your future and your life for a particular purpose. He will make a way to ensure your success. His words do not come back empty or void. When he says you shall overcome, He actually means it. He cannot lie. When He says that you are being tested for His purpose, believe it.

August 20

But God chose what is foolish in the world to shame the wise; God chose what is weak in the world to shame the strong.
1 Corinthians 1:27, ESV

Sister, you must be wise and humble enough to make decisions about the lessons of life that will confront you on a daily basis. Take your lead from our Father. He will shame a person who thinks they have all the answers and uplift a person who has only one unproven answer. He will choose a situation that is weak because it is selected by a few people and neglect one that is favored by the masses. That is the kind of Father we serve and love. He is fair and is not biased toward numbers and masses. So move with patience and wisdom into this day. Be slow to cast shame on those things you once thought foolish and be quick to recognize what is weak and what is strong.

August 21

Give me a sign of your goodness, that my enemies may see it and be put to shame, for you, LORD, have helped me and comforted me.
Psalm 86:17, NIV

Father, you have been my strength when I was weak. You have been my strong tower when I was lost. You have been my rock when I needed a hiding place. I know no other source where I can find everything I need in this world except you. I magnify and praise your holy name. I am happy to know that you are my Father and the lover of my soul. I know you care and have protected me from day to day. But Father, right now, I have a need like David, when his enemies sought him. I have many enemies who want me to fall. Some of them seek my destruction. Father, I, like David, need a sign of goodness from you, so when my enemies see it, they will run and be afraid to approach me again. Thank you, Father, for your protection, comfort, and love. I am blessed to have you in my life.

August 22

Do not forsake wisdom, and she will protect you; love her, and she will watch over you. Proverbs 4:6, NIV

Some people will tell you that knowledge is more important than wisdom or understanding. That may be true for some people who do not know our Father. They put their trust in themselves and believe that they alone have the capabilities of advancing themselves in life. They search for wisdom in books, words, and world leaders. Wisdom is a gift that comes from knowing the Holy Spirit and having Him live within you. As you seek wisdom, get understanding that leads to all truths. Greet this day by loving wisdom and she will protect and cover you when all else fails.

August 23

The LORD is near to the brokenhearted and saves those who are crushed in spirit. Psalm 34:18, NIV

Father, I feel your presence standing beside me. I even feel the lift in your arms carrying me through this brokenness. My heart is so heavy, and the pain is so sharp that it cuts through the center and chambers of my heart. Father, my spirit is crushed; I am at a standstill. I have no desire to move forward with my life. I know you can mend my broken heart, but I have filled it with the love for someone who has taken all the joy and happiness away, and now my heart bleeds and needs to be drained of this bitter love. You are my comfort and my hiding place. You will lift me up out of this valley of despair. Thank you, Father. I know you will save me from this broken state of heart and mind. You will return the joy and happiness I once felt.

August 24

I press toward the mark for the prize of the high calling of God in Christ Jesus. Philippians 3:14, KJV

Come on, sister. Set your priorities in order and get in this press. This press is a good press because it leads to a destination that you have always wanted. It is a move much closer to your hopes and dreams. When you make up your mind that you are moving forward, nothing will get in your path that you will not be capable of moving. Once you can see around the bend and set your sights on the prize, you will run much harder, with finesse, skill, and determination. So get in the race and step up your pace; there are many runners already ahead of you. Your press is not only for your professional progress but most importantly, for the high calling in Christ.

August 25

Truly I tell you the truth, if you have faith as small as a mustard seed, you can say to this mountain, 'Move from here to there,' and it will move. Nothing will be impossible for you. **Matthew 17:20, NIV**

Here is a notable Faith Nugget that can also be called a Truth Nugget. It is a known fact that was stated over two thousand years ago. The veracity of this nugget was just as true and potent then as it is now. If we want to see the evidence of this nugget, we must have more than a belief in something. We must have faith to believe that what we hope for will come to pass. That is the power of faith. Faith and belief work together. The same mountain that was moved over two thousand years ago will move again, even when your faith is as small as a mustard seed. So start using this nugget by asking the Holy Spirit to give you this gift and fruit.

August 26

We are hard pressed on every side, but not crushed; perplexed, but not in despair. 2 Corinthians 4:8, NIV

You are going to always be the object of somebody's seat of oppression because of who you are. When you do not follow the path carved by those who have no regards for truth, they will resort to cruel tactics to stop your growth. Aggressive strategies and cruel tactics are the only methods your enemies will use to try to defeat you. They do not know your Father. If they did, they would be loving and kind toward you. Continue to persevere as you are doing now. You are tormented, but yet you stand. You are detracted, but you remain focused. You are confused, but you are never discouraged. So go into this day as a victor over those who would destroy you.

August 27

And God is able to bless you abundantly, so that in all things at all times, having all that you need, you will abound in every good work.
2 Corinthians 9:8, NIV

Daughter, count the many blessings that have been bestowed upon you. There are many more awaiting you in the future, because I am rich in all things, whether they are in the spirit or physical realm. Your needs will be supplied. I am not slack concerning the promises I have made to you. Your future is already blazed in the path that lies before you. I have already planned and established your place in life. The table is set before you. No force, condition, or situation will change what I have ordained for you. You will be successful in doing every good work your hands will touch. I am your Father and I have declared and decreed these blessings for you.

August 28

And those who know your name put their trust in you, for you, O LORD, have not forsaken those who seek you. Psalm 9:10, ESV

Father, I know your name. I put my trust in you. I have searched in many places looking for someone to care for me and to love me for myself. I know that you will deliver on time. I know you because I have tried you and found you to be my peace in the midst of my storms. You are truth when wrong tries to cover up right, and you are wisdom when foolishness blinds the eyes of the weak. Father, I am walking into this day without any fear, stress, or thoughts of evil overcoming me. I will rejoice and sing praises to you. You are my protector and the lover of my soul. You will not suffer my foot to be moved when danger surrounds me. Your angels will catch me if I fall.

August 29

Keep me as the apple of your eye; hide me in the shadow of your wings.
Psalm 17:8, NIV

Father, I know that this is a day you have given me and I am glad in it, but my heart is so heavy. Sadness and depression are creeping upon me and I need a place to hide from them. I know that I am precious to you because you have kept me safe since my youth. Keep me as the apple of your eye where your sight will always be upon me. I have always loved the shadow of your wings. Let me rest there until this feeling has passed over me.

August 30

Whoever heeds instruction is on the path to life, but he who rejects reproof leads others astray. Proverbs 10:17, ESV

There are always instructions on the road to life. Good instruction is a two-way street. The one who gives it must be sure he is right, and the one who follows it must be sure it is sound. The one who follows good instruction will reach her destination, but the one who rejects it will be lost.

August 31

Let all that you do be done in love.
1 Corinthians 16:14, ESV

Let not your heart be filled with anger or hatred. These things destroy the heart and you will not be able to feel the fruit and gifts of the Spirit. Let what you say and all that you do be done in love. Love is kind, patient, and is not boastful (1 Corinthians 13:4). "Love covers a multitude of sins" (1 Peter 4:8, ESV). As you greet today, love your enemies and do good to those who forsake and do evil to you. Your Father is watching everyone, and He will avenge those who wrong you.

SEPTEMBER

The Hydrangea Flower Symbolizes:
heartfelt emotions, gratitude, boastfulness, bragging, vanity, and apology

September 1

The LORD bless you and keep you; the LORD make his face to shine upon you and be gracious to you; the LORD lift up his countenance upon you and give you peace. Numbers 6:24-26, ESV

Rest peacefully in the assurance that your Father wants the best for you. He has blessed you in the morning, in the evening, and throughout your life. There is nothing He would withhold from you. He has showered favor upon you and placed you in positions where your skills and talents would be used to your advantage, for the advancement of the less fortunate, and for young girls who emulate and follow in your footsteps. Continue to walk with integrity and blessings will shine upon you.

September 2

The LORD repay you for what you have done, and a full reward be given you by the LORD, the God of Israel, under whose wings you have come to take refuge! Ruth 2:12, ESV

Just like Ruth received the favor of our Father over two thousand years ago for being obedient and caring for her mother-in-law, Naomi, the same favor awaits you for your obedience in your Father's service. Walk into today under the wings of your Father. He has you covered.

September 3

Walk in wisdom toward outsiders, making the best use of the time. Let your speech always be gracious, seasoned with salt, so that you may know how you ought to answer each person. Colossians 4:5-6, ESV

Sister, it is important how you present yourself to people who do not know you. You are representing your Father when you walk among people who are still a part of the world. Be polite, but stern in your speech, and careful not to compromise your beliefs and convictions. The first impression you leave with people is usually a lasting one and most people do not have a second chance to change it. But if the second chance presents itself, you will know what to say and how you should respond to each person. So greet today with the knowledge that wisdom will find a way to correct ways of reproach and grant approval to adverse conditions.

September 4

When pride comes, then comes disgrace, but with the humble is wisdom. Proverbs 11:2, ESV

Always walk humble with everyone and never place yourself above others. Seek to find common ground with all people before deciding if they are worthy of your conversations. Placing yourself on a pedestal is a high place to maintain for the rest of your life. The distance you will have to travel if you should fall will cause great harm to your character. Live in such a way that no one will have cause to question your integrity or your character. Be wise and move in circles where you feel comfortable and not required to obligate yourself to others. When the time presents itself, your Father will open doors for you and all you have to do is just be faithful and walk through them.

September 5

I know how to be brought low, and I know how to abound. In any and every circumstance, I have learned the secret of facing plenty and hunger, abundance and need. Philippians 4:12, ESV

Life is not always colored in black and white. There are some grey areas that are difficult to get through and there are choices you will have to make. These areas have less highs and many more lows. You must know how to survive the lows and rise above them and not allow yourself to be buried in the dredges of self-pity and scorn. You have been brought low before and you have bounced back with more determination to succeed, and succeed you did. You have lived when there were days when the pantry was filled with food and you had no need for anything because your Father supplied all your needs according to His riches in glory. So rise up and walk in grace and faithfulness. Your Father will never forsake you.

September 6

Truly, truly, I say to you, whoever receives the one I send receives me, and whoever receives me receives the one who sent me.
John 13:20, ESV

Sister, do not be so quick to turn your back on this person. Remember that our Father sends those in need to us to test our faith and observe the practice of His precepts toward others. It is written that sometimes we are in the company of angels and are not aware that they have been sent by our Father to see if we will accept them or turn them away. He has said that when we minister to them, we minister to Him; and when we receive them, we receive Him. So let us rejoice when we see our sister in need. When we help her, we receive our Father.

September 7

Not neglecting to meet together, as is the habit of some, but encouraging one another, and all the more as you see the Day drawing near. Hebrews 10:25, ESV

Sister, the times in which we live now require more gatherings of believers in our Father. We must uplift each other and encourage our neighbors and loved ones to be strong in our Father's love and protection. These meetings will strengthen us and increase our faith so that we will be able to face anything that will come before us. There is strength in numbers. When more people pray, more petitions will reach our Father's ears and will cause Him to show mercy toward us. His grace will abound upon us and erase our fearful hearts. So go prayerfully into this day with our Father's name upon your lips.

September 8

Without counsel plans fail, but with many advisers they succeed.
Proverbs 15:22, ESV

How do you expect to accomplish the things you have thought about or the things you have held in your heart for years without a plan? How can you succeed unless you talk with someone who has traveled the road you will travel or walk in the shoes they have walked in? Without a plan or any counsel, you will surely fail. Seek instructions from those who are wise and have walked many paths that led to success. Have you even talked with your Father? He sees all things and knows what is in our future. Seek His face about this matter. He knows you more than any person on this earth. So arise and greet this day with a satisfied mind that all your desires and wants will be met. Your Father is faithful to those who are faithful to Him.

September 9

Above all, keep loving one another earnestly, since love covers a multitude of sins. 1 Peter 4:8, ESV

Stop measuring a person's love by their looks and what they wear. You will never know the actual worth of a person by weighing their outward appearances. Looks are deceiving and have caused many people to make wrong choices in life. Look within the person's heart and see what issues from the soul they have, rather than the surface of a person. Love that is pure, honest, and upright will survive all kinds of faults seen in a person. If there are any faults, do not try to erase them, overlook them, or even attempt to fix them. Let your Father, who is the architect and builder of character and integrity, reshape and mold them into what He wants them to be. So greet this day by loving them with a sincere and faithful love.

September 10

For we walk by faith, not by sight.
2 Corinthians 5:7, ESV

When someone asks how you are walking, tell them you are walking with your spiritual mind. Your paths are always clear and not filled with clutter. Let them know that you are walking with a made-up mind that is fixed on your Father, His Son, and His Holy Spirit. A made-up mind allows God to direct your paths and tell you where and when to walk. Tell them that this is how you are able to walk by faith and not by sight. Let them know that this is also how you are able to call things into existence that were never there. So walk into today with a mindset that you will accomplish all and every task that is set before you.

September 11

Then Miriam the prophetess, the sister of Aaron, took a tambourine in her hand, and all the women went out after her with tambourines and dancing. Exodus 15:20, ESV

Sister, there is nothing wrong with praising our Father with dancing and instruments. Look at what Miriam, Moses and Aaron's sister, did. She placed the instrument in her hand and began to dance. All the women in the wilderness followed her with instruments in their hands. These women were faced with indecisions as they left everything behind. They did not know what was ahead of them, but in their times of wavering and fear, they took the time to give thanks and praise in their own personal and emotional way. So dance in the spirit as these women danced. Our Father loves it when we dance and give Him praise.

September 12

And when you do ask, you do not receive, because you ask with wrong motives, that you may squander it on your pleasures.
James 4:3, BSB

Take notice of how you ask your Father for blessings. So many people do not receive what they ask for because they are asking for all the wrong reasons. These people are blocking their own blessings by being selective in how they will use their blessings. They are called blessing blockers because they ask for blessings that will benefit their personal gain rather than satisfying their needs. They are surprised and upset when other people receive their blessings and they do not. So be encouraged as you approach this day. Your Father will supply all of your needs because you do not ask inappropriately or waste your blessings.

September 13

"Remember, LORD, how I have walked before you faithfully and with wholehearted devotion and have done what is good in your eyes." Isaiah 38:3, NIV

Father, I have loved you since the time I knew how to call your name. I have been faithful in distressful times as well as peaceful times and you came to my rescue. You have been a bridge for me when I had to cross from boundary to boundary in my professional work. Sometimes I was underwater. You lifted my head up to see above the waves. Then you placed my feet on a solid foundation. I know no other source or friend I can turn to when I am sad, happy, or in need. Therefore, I will go into this day without fear or insecurity. I will not even ask you to guide me as I approach this door in my life, because I know you will be there to open it for me. And if it does not open, Father, it is well with my soul, for you have opened so many doors for me.

September 14

I have put my words in your mouth and covered you with the shadow of my hand. Isaiah 51:16, NIV

My precious daughter, let not your heart be troubled over this matter. Have I not been there for you in the past to give you strength? Did I not protect you on the highways and carry you to and from your place of work? I will be there at this appointed time as well. I will place words in your mind and all you will have to do is open your mouth and I will speak through you. You are special to me and I will never let you down. My hand is always stretched out over you to cover you from the wind, the rain, and those who would harm you. I am your protector and your voice when you are not able to speak. Go gracefully into this day with my right hand covering you.

September 15

But he was wounded for our transgressions, he was bruised for our iniquities: the chastisement for our peace was upon him; and with his stripes we are healed. Isaiah 53:5, KJV

My dear daughter, I feel your pain and the brokenness in your voice as you cry out to me. I am here with you. I promise that I will never leave you. Just call my name and the pains in your body will leave. I have been bruised, and I died for your pains over two thousand years ago on an old rugged cross. My body was taken to a tomb and sealed. There were guards placed in front of the tomb. But early that Sunday morning, I took the sting out of death. Victory was taken from the grave and I got up from the grave. Because I got up, by my stripes you are healed. So go into this day shouting that your Savior and Brother lives. Your pains are gone, and because I live, you can face tomorrow.

September 16

Hezekiah turned his face to the wall and prayed to the LORD.
Isaiah 38:2, NIV

Sister, come and witness this Healing Nugget. Hezekiah was the king of Judah, the Southern kingdom of Israel. He observed the capture of Jerusalem, the Northern kingdom of Israel by Assyria, which is now Turkey and Iraq. Hezekiah gave the gold from the temple in Judah to the king of Assyria so he would not be captured. He was sick with a boil that inflamed his body. He was told by the prophet Isaiah to get his house in order for he would die. Hezekiah turned his face to the wall and began to pray. Our Father heard his cry and changed His mind. He told Hezekiah that on the third day he would be healed. Hezekiah had an abscess in his mouth that burst on that third day and he was healed, and fifteen years were added to his life. So, sister, our Father will change His mind about sickness and heal our bodies.

September 17

The LORD makes firm the steps of the one who delights in him; though he may stumble, he will not fall, for the LORD upholds him with his hand. Psalm 37:23-24, NIV

Sister, your walk with our Father is firm and secure. No one or any condition will remove you from your position with Him. Your body may be weary and you may not be able to walk, but your place and steps will remain in the same place. Your Father will walk with you. He will even carry you if you should fall. Your work has been faithful and delightful to Him. He will uphold you in all your ways with his right hand. So walk peacefully into this day with delight. Your Father is true to his words and they will never come back empty or void.

September 18

Jesus looked at them and said, "With man this is impossible, but not with God; all things are possible with God." Mark 10:27, NIV

Daughter, I do not ask much from you, but only that you have faith and believe in me. It is impossible to please me without having faith in me. I am true to my word. Man will promise you the moon and the stars knowing they are not his to give away. I hung them in the heavens and gave them light to bright up the sky as an ocean of gemstones. All things are possible, if only you would believe in me and follow me. Wake up to a new day believing that all your impossibilities will be possible. I will never lead you astray or to places where I cannot protect you. You are safe in my care. Believe in me, and life with abundant blessings await you.

September 19

For he will command his angels concerning you to guard you in all your ways. Psalm 91:11, NIV

You are never alone. There are always angels from your Father's kingdom watching over you. When you were born, your Father assigned three angels to follow you everywhere you go. There is a guardian angel to guide your pathways, a warring angel to fight your battles, and a ministering angel to take care of your pains and griefs. These angels will never leave you. So many people walk through life not knowing that there is help for them when they are in trouble. All they have to do is call upon these angels and they will be there to help them. Go forward into this day leaping for joy and praising your Father that He saw your goodness and did not take your angels away from you. They will be close by to help you.

September 20

People don't light a lamp and put it under a bucket; they put it on a lampstand. Then it gives light to everybody in the house.
Matthew 5:15, NTE

Who can see your works when they are placed in an unknown area or if you continue to hide them from public view? Set them in the open so people may see your good works and applaud you for your skills and talents. People who hide their work are ashamed of their efforts or the works themselves. Be bold and come out of the shadows so your works will be made known. Lift your work up high so the light will fall upon you and your work. Your work will give off a bright light that will serve as a lamp for those who need a light to guide their paths.

September 21

"You are the God who sees me."
Genesis 16:13, NIV

Father, there is nothing that can be hidden from you. You see all things, you know all things, and you are over all things. You are greater than any god on earth and in the entire universe. Nothing escapes your view. The entire world is in your control. You can touch any part of it at will and create calm or disaster. You know the hiding place of every person and their deepest secret. Your eyes see the morning mist as it falls upon the flowers in the meadow. It watches the baby deer racing behind its mother through the woodlands. You see me when I lay down to sleep at night and look after me when I awaken in the morning to see another day. Father, I am glad you see all, know all, and are over all.

September 22

Rejoice in the Lord always. I will say it again: Rejoice!
Philippians 4:4, NIV

Look around and see all the good things you have received. What about the promotions, the increase in pay, and the favor your Father has placed upon your family and loved ones? If that is not enough, think about the number of times you have cried out to Him and He did not waste any time coming to your rescue. Who would not serve a God like this? He is always there for you and has never let you down. Rejoice and be exceedingly glad. Great are your rewards in heaven. Sister, He is your source of help and your reason to rejoice. Get up singing His praises and glorifying His name. Go into this day singing a glad and happy song, rejoicing that your Father is still on the throne.

September 23

Continue steadfastly in prayer, being watchful in it with thanksgiving.
Colossians 4:2, ESV

Sister, we cannot expect to live from day to day and think that whatever we receive is from our own ingenuity. We must stop at some point and realize that all of the good things that are happening in our lives are the result of someone guiding our minds and making decisions for us. Yes, sister, there is someone looking over us, and we owe Him everything – our homes, our jobs, our future, and our lives. We need to let Him know that we are thankful for all He has done for us. We ought to always pray and give our Father thanks for how he has allowed us to walk peacefully on His earth. Father, we thank you for each day.

September 24

Then the Lord knows how to rescue the godly from trials, and to keep the unrighteous under punishment until the day of judgment.
2 Peter 2:9, ESV

My dear child, stop pacing the floor and wondering how you will get through this situation. I am here to take care of you and see you through this struggle in your life. I see, hear, and know all things that happen within this world. You have done no wrong. The only thing you have done was to speak truth as you saw it. Different people see truth in different ways. This is why you are faced with this trial. I know your heart and what you were thinking when you spoke these words. I will defend you, not because you are my daughter, but because you are faithful and worthy of this rescue. So walk into this day proud and secure in your place in this world and life beyond this earth.

September 25

You will be enriched in every way to be generous in every way, which through us will produce thanksgiving to God.
2 Corinthians 9:11, ESV

This Bold Nugget should give you encouragement to go forward and do what you have been called to do. Very few people have the opportunity to exceed twice in different areas. Why are you being reluctant? Your Father has opened this door for you and has set up the stage and even given you what to say and do. What more do you need? Your Father is showing you how to bless and praise Him by rewarding you with riches beyond your imaginations. He knows the way. Why not trust Him? Go forward into this day with joy and the blessings of your Father. He will guide you and spread a table of goodness and prosperity before you.

September 26

Isaac planted crops in that land and the same year reaped a hundredfold, because the LORD blessed him. Genesis 26:12, NIV

Never neglect to give blessings back to your Father for the many rewards and deeds of prosperity He has bestowed upon you. In doing so, you will fulfill the law of the tithe. Plant a seed every now and then toward a good cause and watch how your blessings will return back to you. Look what happened to Isaac. Take a lesson from him. His faithfulness to our Father produced a hundredfold when he reaped the rewards of his work. So greet this day by tithing to a special cause in service, money, or whatever the Spirit of your Father places on your heart. Whatever you decide to give will be a blessing toward the building of your Father's kingdom here on earth. Such a response will please Him and put a smile on His face.

September 27

See to it that no one takes you captive by philosophy and empty deceit, according to human tradition, according to the elemental spirits of the world, and not according to Christ. Colossians 2:8, ESV

Be very cautious when people invite you to participate in activities that go against your training and your precepts. If they do not enhance the future of your profession or your mental or emotional growth, then avoid them. Such activities are designed to deceive you and cause you to lose your integrity and trust in your Father. Be wise as an owl and humble as a dove when in the company of such people. Go into this day looking for truth and understanding to go before every step you take and guide you into peaceful and loving company.

September 28

"For the mountains may depart and the hills be removed, but my steadfast love shall not depart from you, and my covenant of peace shall not be removed," says the LORD, who has compassion on you.
Isaiah 54:10, ESV

Precious daughter, let me tell you about my love for you. Before the time I called my servant Isaiah and gave him words to prophesy to my people, I have loved you. Since that time, new mountains have formed, lakes and streams have changed their course, and rivers and seas have increased in depth and width. My love for you will never cease or depart from my heart. I have placed it in your heart so that when you need me all you have to do is look within yourself and you will find me there. So go forth with faith, hope, and love following you as you walk. All these gifts are wonderful and will bring you joy, but the greatest of these is love. Love is kind and patient, and it will last in spite of hardship, danger, and even death.

September 29

May the LORD give strength to his people! May the LORD bless his people with peace! Psalm 29:11, ESV

Sister, rejoice because your Father has placed added strength in your body. He has given you a strong willpower to overcome many circumstances and oppositions in your future. He has removed barriers that have separated you from receiving the things you have worked so hard to achieve. There will be no more trials of your wisdom or tests of your understanding. All of these restrictions have been removed. You will walk in peace and show love toward others who cross your paths.

September 30

Since we live by the Spirit, let us keep in step with the Spirit.
Galatians 5:25, NIV

Stop straddling the fence by trying to please people. You will never be able to please all the people all the time because some people have different motives and will not be pleased. You have to take a stand as to who you are and who you will trust and believe. Either you will stand for truth and live by it, or you will fall for anything and lose trust in yourself. You have to be real and true to yourself first, before you can be real and true to others. Do not be in a hurry to settle this matter. Talk with your Father and see what He has to say. He will never lead you wrong or into a situation where there will be confusion and distrust. He cares about you and your walk with Him. So walk into today with a skip and a hop in your spirit. That is a walk of confidence and a walk of faith that your Father has already fixed this matter.

OCTOBER

The Marigold Flower Symbolizes:
good fortune, creativity, passion, bravery, courage, and the pot of gold at the end of the rainbow

October 1

And God is able to make all grace abound to you, so that having all sufficiency in all things at all times, you may abound in every good work. 2 Corinthians 9:8, ESV

Our Father is true in all that He has said. He wants to shower you with blessings that you will not have room enough to hold them. His desire is that you will succeed in everything you set your heart to do. He has even carved out roads and paths out of mountains and woodlands for you to tread upon. He is all sufficient in making sure that all your needs are met. So walk triumphantly into this day. Your Father has prepared your way.

October 2

Return to your stronghold, O prisoners of hope; today I declare that I will restore to you double. Zechariah 9:12, ESV

Shout for joy. Go back to the place where you were safe and secure. Hope for tomorrow is on the way. Your Father has promised to give back everything that was taken from you. You will gain back your health, your finances, your job, and more than you can contain. Give your Father praise for doubling your lost. So go into today with prosperity, health, and happiness walking before you. You are the victor.

October 3

Honor the LORD with your wealth and with the firstfruits of all your produce; then your barns will be filled with plenty, and your vats will be bursting with wine. Proverbs 3:9-10, ESV

Do you remember reading how the Levites cared for the temple twenty-four hours around the clock? They did not work in the fields like the other tribes. The other tribes had to bring a portion of the fruits of their crops to the temple to feed them. In return, your Father increased the wealth of the people and the Levites for their obedience in keeping the temple opened for the people to worship Him. This portion is called a tithe. This is why we give a tenth of our earning to the church today and in return, we have prospered in health and wealth. So set aside your tenth as you approach the weekend and see how faithful our Father is concerning His word.

October 4

Do you see a man skillful in his work? He will stand before kings; he will not stand before obscure men. Proverbs 22:29, ESV

Let the work you do speak for you. Examine your work to see the quality, style, and skill that have been placed in it so that no one will be able to question the validity of it. Allow no one to touch or handle a personal form of your work without your permission. Your Father is getting you ready for your future and the doors He will open for you will be waiting for your entrance. Your preparation is very important. The people you will meet will be genuine and well prepared to examine and critique your work. So greet this day by standing tall in your belief and your faith. Your Father will lead and guide you into all truths.

October 5

But now, O LORD, you are our Father; we are the clay, and you are our potter; we are all the work of your hand. Isaiah 64:8, ESV

Father, there are times when I do not know who I am or what my purpose is in this world. I stumble to understand why my choices have not brought me peace, happiness, or prosperity in my life. I walk around with no feelings in my body. Sometimes I think that I was born during the wrong time or in the wrong era. I know you made me and created me in your image, but Father, I need a touch from you. I need you to make me over so I can feel that I have a purpose in being here. Father, I need to feel your presence. I feel the warm tears falling down my cheeks. I know that you are here with me. I know you will guide my steps and lead me into green pastures. Thank you for being a Father who loves and cares for me.

October 6

As for these four youths, God gave them learning and skill in all literature and wisdom, and Daniel had understanding in all visions and dreams. Daniel 1:17, ESV

Sister, everyone has a special gift that is given to them from our Father. People who say that a child cannot learn is wrong. They want the child to learn what they know when the things they know may not have been given to them by our Father. Our Father gives wisdom and understanding which cannot be transferred from one person to another person. Knowledge is limited, but there is no limit to wisdom or understanding. The acquisition of wisdom and understanding will open doors to the languages and the minds of children that have been set apart because a person with no wisdom or understanding said they could not be taught.

October 7

According to the grace of God given to me, like a skilled master builder I laid a foundation, and someone else is building upon it. Let each one take care how he builds upon it. 1 Corinthians 3:10, ESV

Sister, walk discreetly and with care as you carry out the profession to which you have been called. The places and steps you are walking in have been treaded by many devoted and master professionals who were trailblazers. The doors you are walking through have been carved by many forerunners who have placed hinges upon them so they swing back and forth. These doors will lead you to higher heights. These master builders were successful because they received grace from your Father to complete their tasks. As you greet today, keep in mind that someone else will come after you, so keep the foundation in place so the next person will have space to add to it.

October 8

So I went down to the potter's house, and there he was working at his wheel. Jeremiah 18:3, ESV

There are times when our Father has to make things simple for us as He did for Jeremiah. He sent Jeremiah to the potter's house to let him see how the pots were made. Jeremiah saw how the clay was placed on the wheel and how the potter worked the wheel. The first vessel made by the potter was scarred, so he threw it away and made another pot that was right. Our Father told Jeremiah that His people were like clay in His hands; He could shape, mold, or cast them aside. The same message is given to us today. Either we obey or be cast aside. So greet tomorrow with a realization that your Father has already done a wonderful work on you.

October 9

There is neither Jew nor Greek, there is neither slave nor free, there is no male and female, for you are all one in Christ Jesus.
Galatians 3:28, ESV

The Unity Nugget places all people on the same plane with our Father. No nation, race, color, or denomination has a claim on our Father. He is the same to all people if they believe in Him and accept Him as their Lord and Savior. It is said that females have no place in an authoritative or leadership position over man, but Apostle Paul says that there is no difference in the eyes of our Father who sees us all as one. Therefore, if we all, males and females, believe this to be true, then there should be no divisions in the workplace, seminary, or the church when it comes to a position of service. So go peacefully into this day being one in the Spirit with all people.

October 10

For the protection of wisdom is like the protection of money, and the advantage of knowledge is that wisdom preserves the life of him who has it. Ecclesiastes 7:12, ESV

The Wisdom Nugget is like money in the bank. It is a defense against destruction, and unlike money, wisdom cannot be burned, lost, or stolen. It cannot be used as an instrument of exchange between countries and people at work. The love of money is the root of evil, whereas the love for wisdom increases knowledge and understanding. When money is exposed by the owner, the result may be death; but when wisdom is exposed, it prolongs the life of the owner. Therefore, get wisdom and understanding to preserve your inheritance. The knowledge in having wisdom is that it gives life to the ones who have it.

October 11

Is anyone among you suffering? Let him pray. Is anyone cheerful? Let him sing praise. James 5:13, ESV

The Healing Nugget is another powerful nugget because it uses faith, fasting, and prayer for it to be effective. Then it requires the elders of the church or people who have a devoted relationship with our Father, His Son, and His Holy Spirit to anoint the sick and offer up prayers. The prayers of the righteous profits the sufferer much because they believe in the precepts and teachings of our Father. The Praise Nugget has no requirements other than that it should be done with a cheerful heart. So go cheerfully into today praising your Father. When praises go up, blessings will come down.

October 12

God sets the solitary in families; He brings out those who are bound into prosperity; But the rebellious dwell in a dry land.
Psalm 68:6, NKJV

Our Father is a wonderful provider for all people, whether they love Him or not. He lets it rain on the just and the unjust. But at the same time, He looks down on the faithful with mercy and grace. He knows the voice of His sheep and will come quickly to aid and deliver them from their trials and tribulations, and from the snares of the enemy. He sees the ones who are bound with financial obligations and rain down blessings and prosperity upon them to bring them out of their bondages. So walk with your head held high. Step up and down with happiness in your walk. Your Father is getting ready to bless you beyond your wildest dreams. Trust Him, because His words do not come back empty or void.

October 13

Ask, and it will be given to you; seek, and you will find; knock, and it will be opened to you. Matthew 7:7, ESV

This is a time when your Father will deliver to you all the things you have asked for. You have looked for Him in your work, in your home, with your friends, and when your enemies were plotting against you. Many times He has heard your knocks. He has even felt the lump in your chest when you wanted to cry and the tears just would not come. There was something inside of you that held you together and would not allow others to see you cry. He has answered your call. He will reward you for your faithfulness, your steadfastness, and your courage. So go into this day with a gentle and joyful heart.

October 14

And Jabez called on the God of Israel saying, "Oh, that You would bless me indeed, and enlarge my territory."
1 Chronicles 4:10, NKJV

God works in mysterious ways, sister. Look at Jabez. His mother bore him in pain and named him out of her sorrow. He lived a horrible life. People shunned him, called him names, and rebuked him. How many times have you faced the same situations and wanted to hide? Jabez turned to our Father in sorrow and prayed to Him to increase his territory. He also asked the Lord to give him a humble spirit so that he could love people and that his enemies would not harm him. Your Father answered his prayers and gave him everything he asked for. You have delighted yourself in Him and you have been a faithful daughter. Therefore, He will not forsake you. So walk into today with the spirit of Jabez and ask your Father to bless you and increase your territory.

October 15

You are my hiding place and my shield; I hope in your word.
Psalm 119:114, ESV

Father, when I am tired and have listened to false accusations, abused with hurtful words, and hard pressed to understand why, I need a place where the wicked will cease from raging and the weary will be at rest. There has always been a hiding place for me under the shadow of your wings and a resting place behind you. You have been a solid rock, a shield, and a refuge for me. You have protected me from my enemies until I am able to regain my hope and go back to fight again. Father, thank you for your precious words. I have found peace, hope, and love in them. Your words comfort and give me strength to finish the race.

October 16

A thousand may fall at your side, And ten thousand at your right hand, But it shall not come near you. Psalm 91:7, NKJV

My precious daughter, nothing will harm or hurt you. Have no fear of the darts that fly by night or the arrow that fly by day. I am here to protect you. I will always cover you with my hand to prevent the enemy from striking a blow against your stance. I will carry you when you are tired. I will pick you up in my arms and comfort you when grief pours its stings of pain upon your heart. I will walk by your side and at your right hand. No matter how many thousands of enemies come at you, they will never touch you. I am always with you, my beloved daughter. I, your Father, will be here to protect you. I formed you and placed my image in you. Run into this day with the wind at your back and the morning sun guiding your path.

October 17

Let us therefore come boldly to the throne of grace, that we may obtain mercy and find grace to help in time of need.
Hebrews 4:16, NKJV

Sister, there is no need to fear your Father. Be still and know that he is your God. Whatever troubles you, there is always a time when you can go before Him and talk to Him. He will in no wise cast you out. It is no secret that He can do anything. What He has done for other daughters, He will do for you. So gather up your courage, buckle up your strength, and go boldly before His throne of grace. He will have mercy on you and will allow you to tell Him what is on your mind. He will help you in anything that you will need, whether it's physical or spiritual food; He has it for the asking. Go into this day with confidence and faith that whatever is on your mind, your Father knows it already and is able to deliver what you need on time. He is an on-time God.

October 18

"LORD, it is nothing for You to help, whether with many or with those who have no power; help us, O LORD our God, for we rest on You, and in Your name we go against this multitude."
2 Chronicles 14:11, NKJV

Father, all power is in your hands. You can destroy, and you can defend. You know the unrighteousness that is upon this land. You have seen the oppression of the poor and the imprisonment of those who try to exercise their inalienable rights. Father, it is more than we can endure. Help us, Father. We know no other name and no other source who has all power to remove and destroy the enemy that has risen up against us and is trying to suppress us. We have no weapons other than your word and your powerful name. Meet us where we are, Lord. We rest on you.

October 19

The LORD has appeared of old to me, saying, "Yes, I have loved you with an everlasting love; therefore with lovingkindness I have drawn you." Jeremiah 31:3, NKJV

Just as I knew my prophet Jeremiah before he was formed in his mother's womb, I saw you before you entered your mother's womb. Just as I loved him then, I love you in the same way. Now that you are here, I have a greater love for you. My Son, who came to earth in my form, laid down His life for you. "Greater love has no one than this, than to lay down one's life for his friends" (John 15:13, NKJV). I am your Friend and your Father. That is why I have said I loved you before you loved me. I have drawn you close to me because of your love for me. Daughter, my love for you is everlasting and it will not change. Trust me for the true words I say.

October 20

And we know that all things work together for good to those who love God, to those who are the called according to His purpose.
Romans 8:28, NKJV

Get up! Do not let the enemy steal your joy. Put a smile on your face. Do not give him any room to feel proud and boastful. This problem may look bad on the outside, but what has happened may be for your good and others' good as well. Never count our Father out. He can take the worse of situations and turn them around for our good, especially for those who love Him and are called by Him for a certain purpose. So be encouraged. Your Father knows your heart and your intentions. Get up and greet this day with joy and love in your heart for the person who is truly responsible for this action. There is an expression that says, "When someone does you wrong, kill them with kindness."

October 21

I was young and now I am old, yet I have never seen the righteous forsaken or their children begging bread. Psalms 37:25, NIV

There have been a number of things that have taken place in this world. Some new and some old. When I consider these things, there is one thing that I must admit. I have never seen anyone living right overlooked in blessings or any of their children going lacking in food, shelter, or clothing. Our Father always takes care of His own. He provides food for the widows, the homeless, and even takes care of the stray cats and dogs. Sister, the God you serve has never let the righteous down nor left them longing for peace or rest. He makes a way for them out of no way. He picks them up when they fall and carries their burdens on His shoulders. You will never find a Father or God like Him. So greet this day by casting all your cares upon Him. He will see you through this day and every day ahead.

October 22

Keep your lives free from the love of money and be content with what you have, because God has said, "Never will I leave you; never will I forsake you." Hebrews 13:5, NIV

Money is good to have. It pays the bills as well as serves as an exchange for goods and other items. But, the "love of money is the root of all evil" (1 Timothy 6:10, KJV). It can become that way when we place so much emphasis on it that it becomes our god and starts to control us. So many people have lost their jobs, their homes, and even their lives because they thought they had to have it instead of going to the source of all income, which is God, the Father. He will supply all of your needs according to His riches in glory. So greet this day with renewed hope.

October 23

Watch your life and doctrine closely. Persevere in them, because if you do, you will save both yourself and your hearers.
1 Timothy 4:16, NIV

Polonius in one of Shakespeare's famous plays, Hamlet, once said, "To thine own self, be true." So often we take so much care to defend the rights and property of others and neglect our own needs. In the process, the other person benefits from our work, while our own work goes lacking in all respects. While you are taking care of other people's business, take care to attend to your own business as well, because your life has value. What you say and do today will greatly affect you tomorrow. So greet this day with optimism and confidence in yourself. Your life is just as important as the person you are working for.

October 24

Those who trust in the LORD are like Mount Zion, which cannot be shaken but endures forever. Psalm 125:1, NIV

Sister, the trust and faith we have in our Father is solid like a rock. There are no cracks or crevices in Him, our Rock. That is why we can hide in Him and find peace and rest in Him for as long as we live. He will sustain us from the wind and rain. He will keep our enemies from finding us. There is no other place on earth that is safe and secure as His mountain. This mountain will protect and shield us from this day and forever more. Many enemies have tried to climb and enter it unworthily but have fallen. Rise up and face this day with gladness and faithfulness. Continue to trust Him and He will always take care of you.

October 25

For it is God who works in you to will and to act in order to fulfill his good purpose. Philippians 2:13, NIV

Take no credit for your good works and the light that shines in your life. Neither claim total ownership of the many accomplishments you have conquered over the years. There is a power higher than you who has chosen you before you were born and ordained you for His purpose. That power is your Father. He is in you and works with you to maintain the levels of proficiencies that you have attained. There is no goal that He is not aware of nor recognition that He was not instrumental in framing or acquiring for you. So as you approach this day, stop and give Him praise for all the things He has done for you. He will carry you to higher heights.

October 26

For you know the grace of our Lord Jesus Christ, that though He was rich, yet for your sake He became poor, so that you through His poverty might become rich. 2 Corinthians 8:9, NASB

Never lose sight of the grace and love of your Savior and Brother, Jesus Christ. He came into this world rich in gold, frankincense, and myrrh. Yet, He never used it to live by because He wanted to live with you and prove His love for you. There were so many opportunities for Him to gain all the riches in the world. But He was not moved by fame, titles, or positions. He never had an earthly home He could call His own. Though He claimed no possessions, you gained prosperity and riches from His poverty. So walk gracefully into this day, rich in blessings, and in the favor and love of your Father. He cares for you enough to sacrifice His life.

October 27

Then he said to me, "This is the word of the Lord to Zerubbabel saying, 'Not by might nor by power, but by my Spirit,'" says the LORD of hosts. Zechariah 4:6, NASB

Daughter, I cherish you and I want only the best for you as I did for my servant Zerubbabel, the governor of Judah, whom I anointed to rebuild the temple of Jerusalem. He complained that the temple would take many years to build. Some said it would take forty-five years, but with my instructions, he did it in three years. You have been given a mighty task that seems difficult and hard. You will discover that it is not by might or power that you will conquer this task, but you shall conquer it by my Spirit. Go forth. This work is already done.

October 28

But by the grace of God I am what I am, and His grace toward me did not prove vain; but I labored even more than all of them, yet not I, but the grace of God with me. 1 Corinthians 15:10, NASB

This Grace Nugget will carry you far in life. It will pave many roads and open a number of doors. No one knew this better than Apostle Paul who encountered hardship and even the bite of a poisonous snake on his journeys. But it was grace that carried him all the way. Learn from Paul who said that he was who he was by the grace of God. Take grace with you when you enter your place of employment. Take it with you when in the company of others. Take it with you when you enter your household. Grace is the unmerited favor of your Father. No one deserves it, but your Father found favor in you because of your faithfulness. Go gracefully into today with peace, kindness, and care. The protection of your Father will guide your walk and carry you should you fall.

October 29

Only be strong and very courageous; be careful to do according to all the law which Moses my servant commanded you; do not turn from it to the right or to the left, so that you may have success wherever you go. Joshua 1:7, NASB

Joshua is reminding some of his warriors of the Success Nugget used by Moses when they conquered nations and kingdoms. Moses encouraged the men to be focused and follow his lead. Joshua tells his men the same thing. As you go forth today, carry this nugget with you. Don't turn to the right or the left. Be strong and of good courage. Your battle is already won.

October 30

What then shall we say to these things? If God is for us, who is against us? Romans 8:31, NASB

Your path is cleared. Your Father has removed all the obstacles. When He is for you, no one shall oppose you. Gather your strength and move forward. There is much work for you to accomplish before you rest.

October 31

Because he has loved me, therefore I will deliver him; I will set him securely on high, because he has known my name.
Psalm 91:14, NASB

Daughter, whatever the cause, or who you shall encounter, I will deliver you. I will bring you out from any pit or snare you may fall in, because you have been faithful to my precepts. I called you out from among many daughters because I know your heart and your soul. But most of all, you know my name.

NOVEMBER

The Chrysanthemum Symbolizes:
happiness, loyalty, and devoted love

November 1

But the fruit of the Spirit is love, joy, peace, patience, kindness, goodness, faithfulness, gentleness, self-control; against such things there is no law. Galatians 5:22-23, ESV

Happiness fills the heart when the fruit of the Spirit lives within you. This fruit is present in all believers, even though nonbelievers do not see it. The sweet odor radiating from you is captivating and others around you will know that you have been in the presence of your Father. This fruit has a drawing effect on others. It will calm those who are in your midst and give them a feeling of love and comfort. Go into this day with a glorious look of victory on your face. There is no law against this gift because there is freedom in it.

November 2

__Not that I am speaking of being in need, for I have learned in whatever situation I am to be content. Philippians 4:11, ESV__

Sister, are you truly satisfied with who you are and where you are? You are blessed, so thank your Father for the peace of mind and love He has given you. Yes, you have needs and wants. But you also know that you could be in a worse state of body, mind, and spirit. You know how it feels to be without and to have the best of things. Meet this day with contentment in knowing that you have a Father who cares about your needs. He is your Provider, your Healer, your Banner, and your Supplier.

November 3

Give thanks in all circumstances; for this is the will of God in Christ Jesus for you. 1 Thessalonians 5:18, ESV

Sister, no matter what circumstance you find yourself in or how happy you are, always pause and magnify your Father's name. Recognize Him for His majesty, His creation, and thank Him for awakening you to see another day. There were so many people were not able to rise this morning. You got up because of His grace and mercy. Thank Him for a day you have never seen before and a day you will never see again. Then, thank Him for your health, your family, your safety, your resources, and all the blessings He has bestowed upon you. Your Father is pleased when you think about Him and realize that without Him, these things would not be possible. Go into this day with a thankful heart. Your Father will reward you for it.

November 4

Make a joyful noise to the LORD, all the earth! Serve the LORD with gladness! Come into his presence with singing! Psalm 100:1-2, ESV

What a wonderful expression of peace and joy you are wearing on your face this morning. You even had a hum and a song on your mind as you went about your daily work. It looks like you are awaiting a day of thanksgiving, and rejoicing in your spirit and your heart. It is a good thing to praise your Father and to be glad that He has shown grace to you and your household all these years. You have been faithful to Him since your youth, and He will reward you openly for your service. Enter this day with praises and thanksgiving. Your Father has high regards for you. He will not forget your love for Him and the way you praise Him, not only with your lips, but with your heart and your soul.

November 5

Restore to me the joy of your salvation, and uphold me with a willing spirit. Psalm 51:12, ESV

Sister, it is a sad thing to lose the favor of our Father. It is even sadder when He takes His Spirit away from us. We walk as if we have no heart or soul. David, when He was going through his years of despair, lost God's Spirit. He had no joy or peace. His enemies oppressed him daily and sought his death. David fell down before his Father and asked Him to give back the feelings of joy and happiness he once felt. You see, sister, there is pleasure in doing wrong. But once the pleasure is gone, guilt and despair come upon the spirit. Stop feeling sorry for yourself and go to your Father. He understands and will restore your place in Him and give you peace. Stop judging yourself. Your judgment will never compare to His forgiveness.

November 6

Lift up your heads, O ye Gates; even lift them up, ye everlasting doors; and the King of glory shall come in. Who is this King of glory? The LORD of hosts, he is the King of glory. Psalm 24:9-10, KJV

Oh, it would be so wonderful to be one of the doors in the house of worship. Then we could worship and praise our Father day and night as the angels serve Him on His throne. These doors lift their heads as they swing back and forth on their hinges to give Him praise. Imagine yourself as one of these doors awaiting the entrance of our Father. Surely, you can forget about your burden for a second to lift your arms and raise your hands before Him. So walk into today as if you were one of the doors singing and giving our Father all the praises that is due Him.

November 7

What shall I render to the LORD for all his benefits to me?
Psalm 116:12, ESV

Father, as I look at my life, all the accomplishments I have received, all the appointments I have maintained, and all the roads I have traveled, I did not do it on my own. You were there every step and every mile of the way. You covered and protected me from the wiles of my enemies and gave me shelter from the storms. There was always food and water to feed me when I grew hungry. Father, you kept me safe. You clothed me when I was naked and found me when I was lost. You set a standard before me where no one could question my devotion toward you. So what can I give you? I am like David who asked the same question. Father, you already own everything above and under the sun. I know what I will give you. I will give you my love, my heart, and my soul. My whole body belongs to you.

November 8

Oh come, let us sing to the LORD; let us make a joyful noise to the rock of our salvation! Psalm 95:2-3, ESV

Sister, come, join in, and celebrate this Joyful Nugget of praise and thanks to our Father. Let us sing a song of His majesty and the beauty of His Holiness. He has done great things. Let us give Him the highest praise. Hallelujah! He is worthy to be praised. He is the Rock of all Ages. Many believers have hidden in Him and have found refuge and strength in Him until they are able to face their enemy. He is the Lily of the Valley and the Bright and Morning Star. The angels bow down before Him and worship Him for His greatness and power. Go into this day singing a song of praise. He is worthy of your praise.

November 9

And they were to stand every morning, thanking and praising the LORD, and likewise at evening. 1 Chronicles 23:30, ESV

The male Levites were members of the twelve tribes of Israel and represented the tribe of Levi. When they became twenty years of age, they stood as keepers and servants of the temple at Jerusalem. They had to follow the same instructions every day until they were in their old age. They held no jobs. Therefore, they and their families depended on the tithes given to the temple from the crops of the tribes. Their day began by thanking and praising God. This thanks and praise represented the entire nation of Israel. Morning and evening, their prayers went out to all people. So as you greet this day, praise your Father. Give thanks for the safety and covering of all people. Then, at the close of the day, praise Him and thank Him again.

November 10

He who dwells in the shelter of the Most High will abide in the shadow of the Almighty. I will say to the LORD, "My refuge and my fortress, my God, in whom I trust." Psalm 91:1-2, ESV

Sister, the place where you live spiritually is desired by every believer. Many people believe, but few are able to make the sacrifices you have made. Your spirit lives in a special place. It is a place where no evil, doubt, or transgression can ever enter. It is a place of comfort, warmth, and safety. Who would not want to live there? Who would not want the protection under His wings? Go boldly into this day feeling the love, care, and protection of your Father. Wherever you go today, your Father will be there watching over you. Whatever you say today has already been approved by your Father. Go forth with confidence in who you are.

November 11

The angel of the LORD encamps around those who fear him, and delivers them. Psalm 34:7, ESV

Sister, you have angels that have been with you through your youth until you became accountable for your own actions. These angels only have charge over believers in our Father, and they will keep you from faltering. Nonbelievers do not have this choice while they are outside of the ark of safety. The greatest angel that can protect you is the Angel of the Lord, which is Jesus Christ, your Savior, and Brother in the Spirit.

November 12

In the day of prosperity be joyful, and in the day of adversity consider: God has made the one as well as the other, so that man may not find out anything that will be after him. **Ecclesiastes 7:14, ESV**

The Prosperity Nugget and the Adversity Nugget oppose each other in the physical world, but complement each other in the spirit realm. The physical realm embraces prosperity while rejecting adversity. We all want to prosper, but no one wants any hardships. The spirit realm causes us to be grateful for adversities because hardships keep us humble and we have to pray daily for deliverance. Our faith is increased during our struggles. Greet this day with a prosperous and humble heart. Your Father watches your steps. He knows your desires, and He will cause you to prosper in all your ways and will comfort you during adversities.

November 13

Whoever gives thought to the word will discover good, and blessed is he who trusts in the LORD. Proverbs 16:20, ESV

The world is such a blessed place to live in when you know your place in it. The blessing is wholly due to finding our place in our Father through His word. His word is sharp; it cuts and it divides. It can mend as well as tear. But the greatest thing about His word is that it has a comforting effect on the bereaved, the hungry, the lost, and those going through oppressions in their lives. Where would you be without His word? You are who you are today because of His word. His word has quickened your spirit and given you strength and courage to move forward. Leap into this day with His word at your sides, in front of you, and in the back of you to push you to levels of greater achievements and growth in His blessings.

November 14

For God so loved the world, that he gave his only Son, that whoever believes in him should not perish but have eternal life.
John 3:16, ESV

Wow! What a sacrifice! How many of us would be willing to sacrifice our son so that the world could be saved? We would not even think about it because the pain of losing our own son would be too great to bear. It is wonderful to know that we do not have to sacrifice our sons for this cause. Furthermore, there is no one who has walked the earth that can compare to the innocence and pureness as His Son. No human or animal can offer eternal life in exchange for the precious blood lost on the cross. Greet this day with the realization that with the sacrifice of His Son's life, your son has a right to the tree of life.

November 15

If I speak in the tongues of men and of angels, but have not love, I am a noisy gong or a clanging cymbal. 1 Corinthians 13:1, ESV

Sister, love is so important and is such a valuable gift to have in your possession. Without it, many hearts would still be cold. Without love, broken hearts would never mend and there would be no such words as kindness or happiness. Love is important because no one can say they have loved unless they love our Father. He is love and has an agape love for everyone. We must have an agape love for Him as well as others. Agape love means loving unconditionally, whether love is returned or not. It means accepting a person, along with all their faults. There is no fear in love. Because there is no fear, we love unconditionally. So approach today with an unconditional love for everyone.

November 16

But he said, "Blessed rather are those who hear the word of God and keep it!" Luke 11:28, ESV

Hearing the words of our Father does not save us, nor does it prevent trials and tribulations from touching or affecting our lives. But it serves as a shield to protect those of us who hear and keep His words. It serves as a fortified wall to block and prevent hateful and envious words of the enemy from destroying our faith. Knowing His words are like a flood that rushes into the heart and erases all the anger and bitterness that's in the world. You are a hearer and a doer of His words; therefore, you are blessed to be called His daughter. Go forth with joy and love in your heart. More blessings than you can count are on their way.

November 17

Blessed are the peacemakers, for they shall be called sons of God.
Matthew 5:9, ESV

People will remember your name when you walk in peace and not in hatred. They will call on you to negotiate or settle indifferences because you give off a pleasant aroma from the Peace Nugget. They can feel the scent of this nugget radiating from your countenance when you enter a room. You are a messenger of peace, love, and happiness. Many young people shall be attracted to you and will want to follow your path. They will be in awe when you speak and search to find any resemblance of the work you have accomplished in your field. So walk humbly and gracefully as you meet this day. There is a broken-hearted, discouraged follower walking behind you who is frightened, disillusioned, and needing healing. Greet him with the peace you have received.

November 18

A man of many companions may come to ruin, but there is a friend who sticks closer than a brother. Proverbs 18:24, ESV

Be weary of people who gather around you in large numbers, all claiming to be your friend. No one has that many friends. A friend is a person that is loyal and trustworthy. You may have many associates, but a friend is few and between; they are hard to find. A person who attracts large numbers in a crowd has something that everyone else wants. When such a large number gathers, there are sure to be some who begrudge you for your accomplishments in life. So as you greet today, move wisely, walk confidently, and be watchful with the spirit of discernment to be able to detect friend from foe.

November 19

I will lift up mine eyes unto the hills, from whence cometh my help. My help cometh from the LORD, which made heaven and earth.
Psalm 121:1-2, KJV

Here comes my help. He comes from afar, but is yet so close. I can see Him in the hills. Even the hills move as He moves. Everything in His path bows down and recognizes His name. He is known by many names: Jehovah Jira, my provider; Jehovah Shalom, my peace; and Jehovah Rophe, my healer. I am so glad I know Him. I know Him as my Father, the lover of my soul. And now I see Him as my Hill, and all of my help comes from my Hill. As I greet this approaching day, I will lift my eyes up to praise my Hill.

November 20

Remind them to be submissive to rulers and authorities, to be obedient, to be ready for every good work. **Titus 3:1, ESV**

Sister, all people who work, even those who are in a supervisory or administrative position have someone that they must listen to. That is what obedience and submission are all about. Apostle Paul tells us to listen to and obey those people in authority, like our local, state, and national leaders and other people we report to. There may be times when we may believe that they are overbearing and unfair. But continue to obey and give it to our Father. When we are obedient, submissive, and faithful, our Father rewards us openly. He blesses those who respond positively to their overseers and supervisors. So make up your mind to persist and obey.

November 21

And let us not grow weary of doing good, for in due season we will reap, if we do not give up. Galatians 6:9, ESV

After overcoming many trials while doing good, more trials are yet to come. You are not out of the woods yet. Trials will come your way as long as there is life in your body. You cannot give in or quit. You must still do good, as the Apostle Paul says. Many people, because they are living in trying times, where world leaders are so unrighteous, choose to live as the world lives. They live as if there is no day of reckoning. We cannot give up; we have to keep pressing our way through. So leap into tomorrow with a stronger faith to do better than ever before. If you go half the way, God will meet you the rest of the way.

November 22

The LORD preserves the simple; when I was brought low, he saved me. Psalm 116:6, ESV

Guard your integrity and personal worth. Do not allow the enemy to read your character by determining who you are and where you are going. Once he has a glimpse of your inner soul, he will carry you to the highest heights and stand on the sidelines, laughing as you fall. Then, as your soul crashes, the enemy will run to collect it and place it in bondage where it will no longer feel the joy of freedom and the love of our Father. Rise up and take charge of the body in which your spirit lives. Wake up and command your soul to recognize the call of your Father. He knows about your burdens and is able to carry all of them. Go forth into today with a made-up mind. Your Father has promised to keep the simple minded safe, secure, and free from the grasp of the enemy.

November 23

Give thanks to the LORD, for he is good, for his steadfast love endures forever. Psalm 136:1, ESV

Our Father is a good and loving God. Pause this morning to give Him thanks for all the blessings He has given to you and your family. Adore Him and magnify His holy name. His angels kept watch over you through the night. He allowed you to rise this morning enclosed in your right mind. He looked in on your family and saw that they were alive and well. Father, you are good in the way you provided food and nourishment for our bodies. You are good in the way you provided clothing and shelter for us. Your goodness and your mercy endure forever. You are good because you kept us from falling in the snares of the enemy. We are happy to enter this day, for we know your goodness will follow us all the days of my life.

November 24

GOD, the Lord, is my strength; he makes my feet like the deer's; he makes me tread on my high places. Habakkuk 3:19, ESV

The strength our Father gives us is like the might found in the feet of the deer as she glides across the meadows. She runs with grace and finesse as she makes her way across the waterway and into the woodlands. She finds shelter there in the cover of hanging branches, and safety in the thicket of the briar bush. She runs with vigor and haste, running to escape the blow and injury of the hunter's weapon. Like the deer, we shall run into tomorrow with the strength and courage from our Father's storehouse. He will lead us into the dawning of Thanksgiving Day, where we shall bless Him with songs of praise and worship.

November 25

Enter into his gates with thanksgiving, and into his courts with praise: be thankful unto him, and bless his name. **Psalm 100:4, KJV**

Oh, what a glorious day to give thanks to our Father. This is a day He has created. A day of praise and a day of worship. Let us thank Him for His sovereignty and His supreme rule over our destinies. Let us bow and give Him honor and exalt Him for the loving God that He truly is. He is our great I Am. He is our High Tower. He is the Bread that is cast upon the waters and finds its way back to feed us when we are hungry. Today, let us walk into His gates lifting our hands and thanking Him for His protection. Then, let's continue into His courts praising Him for His all-knowing powers, His all-seeing eyes, and His encompassing reign over the entire universe.

November 26

Then he said to them, "Go your way. Eat the fat and drink sweet wine and send portions to anyone who has nothing ready, for this day is holy to our Lord. And do not be grieved, for the joy of the LORD is your strength." Nehemiah 8:10, ESV

Just as Nehemiah, the governor of Israel, sanctioned the Feast of Trumpets, the people celebrated the day with joyful singing, fellowship, and renewing their relations with our Father. They had just finished rebuilding the temple at Jerusalem. Ezra, the priest, read to them from the Holy Scriptures while the people wept. It had been seventy years since they heard such holy readings. The people were told to hush their grieving, eat as much food as they could, take the leftovers, and give it to the poor so they may have a celebration of their own.

November 27

O God, we have heard it with our own ears— our ancestors have told us of all you did in their day, in days long ago. **Psalm 44:1, NLT**

Father, you are no stranger to us. We have heard of your glory, your omnipresence, and all the wonders you have performed since the beginning of time. We were told how you parted the Red Sea, how you closed the lion's mouth, how you opened the tomb, and closed the door to hell. There is nothing that we do not know about you. We know even more about you now because there is a cloud of witnesses who surround us to tell us about your strength and healing. We have felt your presence and know that you are an "I will God." We will greet this day knowing that you will do above and exceedingly all the things you have promised to do.

November 28

Through you we push back our enemies; through your name we trample our foes. **Psalm 44:5, NIV**

We know your power. We know your strength. We have felt your healing. We know how you are a Battle Axe in times of war. How do we know these things? We know them because we have been a receiver of all these things. Father, you are not slack concerning your promises. When you say you will fight our battles, we can depend on it. When you say you will make our enemies our footstool and we will live to see it, that day will surely come. The enemy knows your name. He fears the call of your name and he runs in terror of your presence. Father, deliver us from all of our enemies and cover us under the shadow of your wings. We will go into this day rejoicing that we know your name and you know our name. We will not fear the hand of our enemies nor will we bow to their evil plans. Father, protect us from their ways.

November 29

Let no one deceive you with empty words, for because of these things the wrath of God comes upon the sons of disobedience.
Ephesians 5:6, ESV

Many imposters will come before you claiming to know the seat where your Father sits. They will say vain and empty words to convince you that they know Him. But these words are like water that slides off the feathers of your Father's wings. They have no feeling, no desire, and no intimacy in their meanings. Stay away from people who have an answer for everything and claim to be a discerner of truth and the inner thoughts of the mind. These imposters have no clue to what goes on in their own minds. They are deceivers seeking to rob you of your innocence, your purity, and your truth. Go bravely into this day reversing their words on them by giving them the truth that your Father has given you. Rebuke and reprove them.

November 30

He changes times and seasons; he removes kings and sets up kings; he gives wisdom to the wise and knowledge to those who have understanding. Daniel 2:21, ESV

Come here, sister. Here is a Season Nugget. Our Father is the only one who has the seasons in His hands. He turns the hands of time. He can speed them up, slow them down, and bring them to a complete stop. We can depend on the timing and the days when the seasons will change from spring to summer to fall and winter. He sets up kings and their kingdoms. He tears them down and sets up new ones with new kings. He, in no wise, will withhold wisdom from anyone who seeks it. Run into this day with the source of all wisdom, knowledge, and understanding running alongside of you.

DECEMBER

The Poinsettia Symbolizes:
Christmas, the Star of David, cheer, and success

December 1

The kings of the earth prepare for battle; the rulers plot together against the LORD and against his anointed one. Psalm 2:2, NLT

David sees the future Christ even before His birth. He foretells how the rulers of the earth will bond together to overthrow our Savior, Intercessor, and Brother, Jesus Christ. David foresees how they will strategize and plot the destruction of Jesus. They think that they will destroy our Savior, but little do they know that our Father has a plan to destroy them; and destroy them, He will. As we look around us and beyond, we see this plotting happening now as it happened over two thousand years ago. We have no fear. We believe in the words of our Father. Walk triumphantly into today with no fear of tomorrow. He holds tomorrow, and He holds your hand.

December 2

Commit your work to the LORD, and your plans will be established.
Proverbs 16:3, ESV

Do you want to be successful in life? Do you want a life already planned and laid out? Well, it can all be yours once you decide to commit your work to your Father. Your work is not yours anyway; it belongs to Him. If you have received commissions, rewards, or blessings, it is because of your Father's love for you. So go for the gold and let Him plan it all.

December 3

For the Lord GOD does nothing without revealing his secret to his servants the prophets. Amos 3:7, ESV

When your Father gets ready to make a change in this world, He chooses special people and tells them what He wants the world to know. He can reveal His plans through dreams or visions. He can whisper events in your ears and show you things that have never happened before, and they come to pass. For others, it is a certain feeling they get. Some may see an angelic figure that comes as a messenger. The Father can deliver his message in any way He sees fit. If any of these things have happened to you, then there is a strong possibility that you are a prophetess as Miriam, Deborah, or Anna.

December 4

Rejoice greatly, O daughter of Zion! Shout aloud, O daughter of Jerusalem! Behold, your king is coming to you. Zechariah 9:9, ESV

Our King is coming to us. Make way for the King. Rejoice and be glad. Shout it throughout the hillside. Let the sound of His coming be heard in every home. Take out the banners and raise them high where they can be seen by all the people. Prepare the red carpet, lay out the palm branches, and line the streets with them so He may walk upon them. He is our all and all, our Lord and our Savior. He is our Lily in the Valley and our Bright and Morning Star. So go into today rejoicing that the King of glory is coming in, and when He comes, He will bring life, health, peace, and joy to the world. He will bring love, faith, happiness, wisdom, and understanding to all people who want to know Him and will bless His name.

December 5

Therefore the Lord himself will give you a sign. Behold, the virgin shall conceive and bear a son, and shall call his name Immanuel.
Isaiah 7:14, ESV

The sign they looked for after Isaiah gave this prophecy was the coming of a virgin who would conceive by the Holy Spirit. Even the prophets of old knew of His coming. They prophesied His name "Immanuel, which means 'God with us'" (Matthew 1:23, NLT). They prophesied His arrival, persecution, crucifixion, and untimely death. Isaiah referred to the Messiah as 'The Suffering Servant.' Sister, there is joy for you because He arose from the dead.

December 6

And behold, there was a woman who had had a disabling spirit for eighteen years. She was bent over and could not fully straighten herself. When Jesus saw her, he called her over and said to her, "Woman, you are freed from your disability." Luke 13:11-12, ESV

Wow! What a miracle! Healing can come from just speaking a word of freedom from a crippling spirit. This woman had this complaint for eighteen years. That is a long time to walk bent over with no relief in sight. Imagine the happiness this woman felt when she stood with a straightened body. Sister, because the Father lives in us, we can speak words of healing too. We can pray for a person and healing will come upon that person's body. Your Father has given you many gifts of the Spirit. Start using them. So get up with the spirit of exhortation and greet this day with wisdom and understanding. You will be surprised what He has already planned for your life.

December 7

But when they saw him walking on the sea they thought it was a ghost, and cried out, for they all saw him and were terrified. But immediately he spoke to them and said, "Take heart; it is I. Do not be afraid." Mark 6:49-50, ESV

Sister, I can see in my mind's eye and feel the fear in my heart what these disciples saw and felt when their master walked on the sea. The calm voice of their Messiah relaxed them and took the fear from their hearts. Peter was so confident in His master's voice that He boldly got out of the boat and began to walk toward Him. He was walking briskly until he took his eyes off his master and looked at the crashing waves; he started to sink. Sister, this is a vital lesson for us. The lesson we are to take away is that as we enter this walk of life, we will encounter fears and disappointments. But as long as we keep our eyes on the Messiah, we will overcome our fears and inadequacies.

December 8

The tongue has the power of life and death, and those who love it will eat its fruit. Proverbs 18:21, NIV

The tongue can be a dangerous part of the body. Some people say it should be bridled, many say it is a deadly sword, while others say it is a weapon because it can kill. A body part as small as the tongue has so much power. Since you know that it does, you should be careful what you say. A word spoken in anger can hurt a person, while a word spoken in love can heal a wounded heart. When you love to hurt others, the pendulum of life will one day swing your way causing you pain or even death. So go into this day with a tongue that will sing praises, speak truth, and glorify your Father which is in heaven.

December 9

And keep the charge of the LORD your God, walking in his ways and keeping his statutes, his commandments, his rules, and his testimonies, as it is written in the Law of Moses, that you may prosper in all that you do and wherever you turn. 1 Kings 2:3, ESV

When you commit your life to your Father, you have a charge to keep and a God to glorify. It does not mean that you should give up anything. When you say yes, He will slowly begin to take away bad habits from you. The next thing you know they are all gone, and you will not know when they left. When you give due diligence to Him, He will give more than due diligence to you. Many have tried Him and have found Him to be a lasting friend who will stick closer than a brother. Nothing is too hard for Him when you belong to Him. So call Him up. He will get you through your problems and will prosper you in all your ways.

December 10

And the angel answered her, "The Holy Spirit will come upon you, and the power of the Most High will overshadow you; therefore the child to be born will be called holy—the Son of God."
Luke 1:35, ESV

Mary was surprised to see an angel standing in her room. He told her to have no fear and that he was sent to bring her news of great joy. He told her that she had been chosen by our Father to give birth to His Son. Mary asked him how this thing was going to take place because she knew no man. Then the angel told her the Holy Spirit would come upon her and the power of our Father will cause her to conceive and give birth to a holy child. The key to this Holy conception was belief. Mary had to believe that it would happen. She never denied the angel control of her body. A lesson to learn is when God chooses you for a task, never doubt Him; just believe. Go into tomorrow believing that "with God all things are possible" (Matthew 19:26, KJV).

December 11

But the angel said to her, "Do not be afraid, Mary; you have found favor with God." Luke 1:30, NIV

Sister, it is a glorious thing to have the favor of your Father upon your life. Everything you touch will be blessed. Everywhere you go, doors will open, and people will receive you in love. Many people seek His favor but are not able to find it because they are not looking for Him. They are looking for only what they can receive from Him. Mary was not looking for Him; He found her. She had no idea that the favor that would be placed upon her was to bear a son who would later become her Lord and Savior. So greet this day with gladness in your heart that Mary received the message from the angel. Had she not received it, His favor and that of His Father would not have been passed down to us.

December 12

Every good gift and every perfect gift is from above, coming down from the Father of lights, with whom there is no variation or shadow due to change. James 1:17, ESV

This is the season of the year when people will be buying gifts and exchanging gifts with one another. Some will be pleased, while others will be displeased and will make plans to carry their gift back to the store in exchange for another gift or the money that purchased the gift. So many people will forget the reason for the season and will focus on the material gift rather than the spiritual gift. The true gift is the good and perfect gift that comes from our Father. This gift ranges from wisdom to faith, discernment of spirits, healing, prophecy, speaking in tongues, interpretation of tongues, and miracles. Seek to find the good and perfect gift.

December 13

Give, and it will be given to you. Good measure, pressed down, shaken together, running over, will be put into your lap. For with the measure you use it will be measured back to you. **Luke 6:38, ESV**

Sister, the Measure Nugget is important when it comes to deciding the amount of substance that should be given or received. It is evident that we tend to give more substance to those we love rather someone we randomly meet. But the idea is that we should give the same amount of substance to all people, regardless of their race, creed, or color. Luke says it best when he asks us to give and it will be given to us. He also said that we should be careful how we give. If we give little, we should expect little in return. When we give in good faith, we will receive in abundance. So as you greet today, give a good measure to receive a good measure.

December 14

And Mary said, "My soul magnifies the Lord, and my spirit rejoices in God my Savior." Luke 1:46-47, ESV

After Mary spoke to the angel and received the message that was sent to her, she immediately started lifting the name of our Father. Sister, when you know you have received a blessing that is greater than all the other blessings (not negating any blessings), your heart overflows with thanksgiving, praises, and words of adoration. This praise and magnification came from her soul and spirit first, then traveled to the outer surface of her body and placed a smile on her face and a shout from her mouth. That is what magnification does to the heart; it erupts and flows to the surface. So enter this day magnifying your Father for all the things He has done in your life and the things He will do in the future.

December 15

Their idols are like scarecrows in a cucumber field, and they cannot speak; they have to be carried, for they cannot walk. Do not be afraid of them, for they cannot do evil, neither is it in them to do good.
Jeremiah 10:5, ESV

Our Father encourages Jeremiah to be strong when the evil rulers sent their prophets to frighten him by telling him what their gods would do to him. Do you see how these idol gods are described? They are called scarecrows, which means they have no heart or soul. He said they cannot talk or walk; they have to be carried. Our God is a living God. He speaks. He walks. He has great powers. He sees all, knows all, and is everywhere at the same time. These idol gods can do no evil nor the people who carry them. Your Father is in control. So stop allowing people to control your thoughts by telling you what evil will befall you. Go into this day fearlessly and confidently. Your Father has you covered on all sides.

December 16

One person esteems one day as better than another, while another esteems all days alike. Each one should be fully convinced in his own mind. The one who observes the day, observes it in honor of the Lord.
Romans 14:5-6, ESV

Never compare one day with another day in worth or grace. Consider them all worthy and full of grace. The same God who blesses each day is the same God who created each day. Each day is presented to you for your pleasure, and has a new outlook, and a new promise. Each day should be observed as a blessing from Him and should be honored accordingly. So as you greet this new day, give thanks to the creator and maker of all things. No two days are the same; however, our Father is the architect of all things found in each day.

December 17

But seek first the kingdom of God and his righteousness, and all these things will be added to you. Matthew 6:33, ESV

Are you looking for love, joy, peace, and happiness? These things will never be found in the world because they did not come from the world. The world cannot give something it did not create. It cannot feel something it did not embrace. How can a person know love when they do not love themselves? How can a person have joy and peace when they do not know where they come from? And finally, how can a person find happiness when they do not have it in their own lives? These traits are the fruit of the Spirit and comes from knowing your Father. So seek Him, and all these things shall be added to you.

December 18

"My Spirit that is upon you, and my words that I have put in your mouth, shall not depart out of your mouth, or out of the mouth of your offspring, or out of the mouth of your children's offspring" says the Lord, "from this time forth and forevermore." Isaiah 59:21, ESV

The Inheritance Nugget is meant to ensure that the words of our Father lives forever. His desire is that it will continue to survive as a living source in the hearts and minds of generations to come. Therefore, we must train our children to love the word. We must be real about our love in the presence of others. We must show the love of our Father in our homes, in our talks, and in our living so that the word and the Spirit of our Father will be sealed in their hearts, and the knowledge of His holiness will be passed down from their children to other children branching out from the family tree. So meet today by making up your mind to pass the messages you receive when the Holy Spirit quickens your spirit, down the generational line of your family tree.

December 19

For though by this time you ought to be teachers, you need someone to teach you again the basic principles of the oracles of God. You need milk, not solid food. Hebrews 5:12, ESV

The Teaching Nugget is an appropriate way to spread the truth that God gave His prophets to give to His people. But in order for the truth to be taught without error or flaws, those who will serve as instructors must themselves be taught. Proverbs 27:7 says, "Iron sharpens iron," which means that the master teacher must be someone who is knowledgeable, equipped, and able to convey these facts to a similar group of teachers who were once on solid food but now must return to milk. This is like a student sitting at a desk rather than a podium. So if you are thinking about being a teacher, make sure you drink the milk before eating the meat.

December 20

Behold, the days are coming, declares the LORD, when I will raise up for David a righteous Branch, and he shall reign as king and deal wisely, and shall execute justice and righteousness in the land.
Jeremiah 23:5, ESV

Sister, start making preparation for the arrival of a righteous leader who will not focus on himself but will place the peoples' needs before his needs. He shall declare a new nation and decree that all people are equal. He will love all people, all races, and strive to maintain liberty and justice for all. The land will be free and will bring forth its fruit to feed the masses. So rejoice and be exceedingly glad. Our Father will raise up a leader who is a wise judge to lead His people out of oppression, imprisonment, and unrighteousness. The days of uncertainty, harassment, and neglect will soon come to an end. The people will shout with joy. They will run into the streets and sing praises to our Father.

December 21

Now there are varieties of gifts, but the same Spirit; and there are varieties of service, but the same Lord; and there are varieties of activities, but it is the same God who empowers them all in everyone.
1 Corinthians 12:4-6, ESV

Do not think that you have a special gift that no one else has. All gifts come from the same source. That source is the Holy Spirit. Some people have talents or skills, such as typing more words per minute than the average typist. A skill or a talent is acquired through practice or sometimes comes innately. There are several spiritual gifts, such as the gift of wisdom, faith, exhortation, teaching, serving, giving, and leadership to name a few. All of these gifts are from the Holy Spirit who gives freely to anyone who asks in sincerity. So if you have a gift or a talent, use it for the glory of your Father and not for personal gain.

December 22

Blessed is she who has believed that the Lord would fulfill his promises to her. Luke 1:45, NIV

Mary went to see her cousin Elizabeth who lived in the hillside country of Judea. Elizabeth was with child in her old age, and Mary went to inquire about her health. When Elizabeth heard Mary's voice speaking to her husband Zacharias, the priest, the baby leaped in her womb and the Holy Spirit, who was not in the world yet began to speak through Elizabeth and gave Mary blessings and salutations. Elizabeth's baby was later called John the Baptist, who was a forerunner of Jesus. The Holy Spirit in Elizabeth as well as the baby in Elizabeth's womb recognized the future baby King in Mary's womb. So if Christ is in you, the Holy Spirit will know your name.

December 23

And Mary said, "My soul magnifies the Lord, and my spirit rejoices in God my Savior." Luke 1:46-47, ESV

When favor is showered upon you, the joy felt is the same joy Mary felt when she found favor with our Father. He had chosen her among all the women in the world to conceive and give birth to His Son. What a wonderful and glorious day to know that you have been chosen by God Himself. God chose you to be the mother of your son or daughter. Jesus was not only the Savior of the world, but Mary's Savior too. She had a reason to rejoice. She has a permanent place in the archives of history. So greet this day rejoicing and praising your Father that He has found favor in you and allowed you to rise this morning to see another day.

December 24

And in the same region there were shepherds out in the field, keeping watch over their flock by night. Luke 2:8, ESV

The night when our Father's Son was born so was the Joy Nugget. There were shepherds resting in the field under the open sky. The sheep were also resting and awaiting the dawn of a new day. The fields were close to the city of Bethlehem where the baby King was rumored to be born. When the night sky was so bright and lit up with dancing stars, an angel appeared to them. The angel told them to fear not, for on this night a Savior would be born who is Christ the Lord (Luke 2:10-11). The angel told them where to find the baby and that peace would come to the world. Immediately, they heard heavenly voices singing praises to our Father. So on this night, pray for peace and joy in the world, and that you will awake to a new birth, a new freedom, and a new life.

December 25

When the angels went away from them into heaven, the shepherds said to one another, "Let us go over to Bethlehem and see this thing that has happened, which the Lord has made known to us."
Luke 2:15, ESV

The shepherds were so excited and mystified that they decided to go to Bethlehem to see if what the angels said had truly come to pass. When they got there, they found the child wrapped in a blanket of folded cloth, lying in a feeding trough for animals. They rejoiced at the glorious sight. They worshipped and bowed before Him. When they left, they told what they had seen to all the world, as many wondered if it was true. There are so many people today, sister, who still doubt His birth. Blessed are those who have not seen Him but yet believe in Him. So as you rejoice today, never forget the reason for the season. The Messiah will never ever forget you. He is your Savior, your Intercessor, and your Brother in the Spirit.

December 26

And the Word became flesh and dwelt among us, and we have seen his glory, glory as of the only Son from the Father, full of grace and truth. John 1:14, ESV

The Word had been here since the world was framed. The Word spoke the world into existence. The Word placed His image into the first man, Adam. The Word was present throughout the Old Testament until our Father made His Son flesh to come to earth to redeem mankind back to Himself. He was in the world, but the world knew Him not. He came to His own and His own received Him not. But as many as received Him, to them He gave eternal life and the right to become His sons and daughters. The world had Him and all His glory but could not love or receive Him. So greet this day with joy and grace. You have been grafted into the branch of the family tree. Because God is your Father, His Son has become your Brother.

December 27

"Where is He who has been born King of the Jews? For we have seen His star in the East and have come to worship Him."
Matthew 2:2, NKJV

The wise men were astrologers and saw His star in the east. They followed the star until it rested above the city of Judea. The wise men went to the King Herod, who was also looking for the child. King Herod told the wise men when they find the child to come back and bring him word so he could also worship Him as they do. However, King Herod had another motive for finding the child. He was threatened by the fact that the child was born to rule the world and he wanted to kill the child. So greet today with a spirit of discernment. Everyone does not have the same purpose in life as you. So try the spirit by the Spirit to see if it is of your Father's (1 John 4:1). If it is not, depart quickly.

December 28

And going into the house, they saw the child with Mary his mother, and they fell down and worshipped him. Then, opening their treasures, they offered him gifts, gold and frankincense and myrrh.
Matthew 2:11, ESV

The wise men continued their journey until the star stood directly over the stable where the child lay. They went inside the stable. When the men saw the child, they bowed before Him. They worshipped Him and gave Him precious gifts to honor Him. As they were leaving, an angel came to the men and sent them another route away from King Herod. Beware when people ask you to come back and bring a report instead of going themselves. They have a hidden agenda. So walk with care. Every object that glitters is not your Father's first choice. Sometimes we have to come from the lowest place in society to be appreciated and loved by the masses. This is our Father's way of pruning us before we go out to represent His word. We must be true to Him and know who we are in Him in order to know Him.

December 29

"Be still, and know that I am God; I will be exalted among the nations, I will be exalted in the earth." Psalm 46:10, NIV

My precious daughter, do not let those things around you upset you. You will see and hear many things before I come again. Fret not or be afraid. These things must happen because they are written and recorded. But I will come and remove you from their presence so they will not harm you. Go faithfully into this day. I am always with you.

December 30

Rejoice always, pray continually, give thanks in all circumstances; for this is God's will for you in Christ Jesus.
1 Thessalonians 5:16-18, NIV

When others are sad or even angry, always keep a smile on your face and love in your heart. Have a word of encouragement to give to those in distress and to the lost. Pray for everyone, and no matter what condition you are in, always thank your Father, and life will be kind to you.

December 31

These things I have spoken to you, that my joy may be in you, and that your joy may be full. **John 15:11, ESV**

My darling daughter, I have no desire that you should be lost. I have prepared a way for you and want you to find your way home. I have given you purpose, wisdom, and strength to overcome adversities. I have written these things so you will find peace and happiness in this world. One day you will overcome the world as I have overcame it. So, my dear, I am watching over you. Remember that peace, love, joy, and happiness shall follow you all the days of your life.

SCRIPTURES ON FAITH

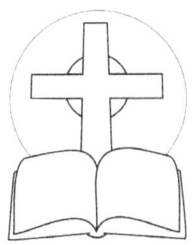

1. Hebrews 11:1, KJV
Now faith is the substance of things hoped for, the evidence of things not seen.

2. Hebrews 11:6, KJV
But without faith it is impossible to please him: for he that cometh to God must believe that he is, and that he is a rewarder of them that diligently seek him.

3. James 1:3, KJV
Knowing this, that the trying of your faith worketh patience.

4. 1 Peter 1:8-9, KJV
Whom having not seen, ye love; in whom, though now ye see him not, yet believing, ye rejoice with joy unspeakable and full of glory: Receiving the end of your faith, even the salvation of your souls.

5. Mark 9:23, KJV

Jesus said unto him, If thou canst believe, all things are possible to him that believeth.

6. 1 John 5:4, KJV

For whatsoever is born of God overcometh the world: and this is the victory that overcometh the world, even our faith.

7. Matthew 21:22, KJV

And all things, whatsoever ye shall ask in prayer, believing, ye shall receive.

8. Mark 10:52, KJV

And Jesus said unto him, Go thy way; thy faith hath made thee whole. And immediately he received his sight, and followed Jesus in the way.

9. Ephesians 2:8, KJV

For by grace are ye saved through faith; and that not of yourselves: it is the gift of God.

10. Matthew 11:23, KJV

For verily I say unto you, That whosoever shall say unto this mountain, Be thou removed, and be thou cast into the sea; and shall not doubt in his heart, but shall believe that those things which he saith shall come to pass; he shall have whatsoever he saith.

SCRIPTURES ON PRAYER

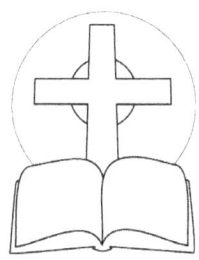

1. Colossians 4:2, NIV
Devote yourselves to prayer, being watchful and thankful.

2. 1 John 5:14, NIV
This is the confidence we have in approaching God: that if we ask anything according to his will, he hears us.

3. Mark 11:24, NIV
Therefore I tell you, whatever you ask for in prayer, believe that you have received it, and it will be yours.

4. Jeremiah 29:12, NIV
Then you will call on me and come and pray to me, and I will listen to you.

5. Romans 12:12, NIV
Be joyful in hope, patient in affliction, faithful in prayer.

6. Psalm 145:18, NIV

The LORD is near to all who call on him, to all who call on him in truth.

7. Jeremiah 33:3, NIV
Call to me and I will answer you and tell you great and unsearchable things you do not know.

8. Hebrews 4:16, NIV
Let us then approach God's throne of grace with confidence, so that we may receive mercy and find grace to help us in our time of need.

9. Matthew 6:6, NIV
But when you pray, go into your room, close the door and pray to your Father, who is unseen. Then your Father, who sees what is done in secret, will reward you.

10. John 15:16, NIV
You did not choose me, but I chose you and appointed you so that you might go and bear fruit—fruit that will last—and so that whatever you ask in my name the Father will give you.

SCRIPTURES ON HEALING

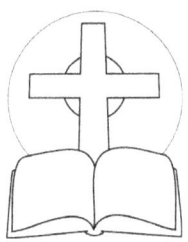

1. 1 Peter 2:24, NLT
He personally carried our sins in his body on the cross so that we can be dead to sin and live for what is right. But his wounds you are healed.

2. Jeremiah 30:17, NLT
"I will give you back your health and heal your wounds," says the LORD.

3. Matthew 14:36, NLT
They begged him to let the sick touch at least the fringe of his robe, and all who touched him were healed.

4. Mark 5:34, CEV
Jesus said to the woman, "You are now well because of your faith. May God give you peace! You are healed, and you will no longer be in pain."

5. Isaiah 53:5, KJV
But he was wounded for our transgressions, he was bruised for our iniquities; the chastisement of our peace was upon him; and with his stripes we are healed.

6. James 5:14, NKJV
Is anyone among you sick? Let him call for the elders of the church, and let them pray over him, anointing him with oil in the name of the Lord.

7. James 5:15, ESV
And the prayer of faith will save the one who is sick, and the Lord will raise him up. And if he has committed sins, he will be forgiven.

8. Deuteronomy 7:15, ESV
And the LORD will take away from you all sickness, and none of the evil diseases of Egypt, which you knew, will he inflict on you, but he will lay them on all who hate you.

9. Matthew 10:8, ESV
Heal the sick, raise the dead, cleanse lepers, cast out demons. You received without paying; give without pay.

10. 2 Chronicles 7:14-15, NKJV
If my people who are called by my name will humble themselves, and pray and seek my face, and turn from their wicked ways, then I will hear from heaven, and I will forgive their sin and heal their land.

BIBLE REFERENCES

Scripture quotations marked (BSB) are from the Berean Study Bible.
Scripture quotations marked (CEV) are from the Contemporary English Version.
Scripture quotations marked (CSB) are from the Christian Standard Bible.
Scripture quotations marked (ESV) are from the English Standard Version.
Scripture quotations marked (KJV) are from the King James Version.
Scripture quotations marked (NASB) are from the New American Standard Bible.
Scripture quotations marked (NIV) are from the New International Version.
Scripture quotations marked (NKJV) are from the New King James Version.
Scripture quotations marked (NRSV) are from the New Revised Standard Version.
Scripture quotations marked (NLT) are from the New Living Translation.
Scripture quotations marked (NLV) are from the New Life Version.
Scripture quotations marked (NTE) are from the New Testament for Everyone.

ACKNOWLEDGMENTS

To the special women pictured on the cover of this devotional – Elizabeth W. Cooley, Megan Hamby, Pamela Rowell, and Martha Ann Whitacre – thank you for allowing me to use your likeness. Each one of you is making a difference in the lives of others. May God continue to provide you with comfort, encouragement, and inner strength.

 Elizabeth W. Cooley is a wife, mother, grandmother, and a licensed agent at Senior Solutions of South Carolina, Inc.

 Megan Hamby is a Patient Care Technician. She enjoys working out, singing, and gardening.

 Pamela Rowell is a science teacher with over 20 years of experience in education, a licensed minister, and co-founder of *Love and Truth Ministries*.

 Martha Ann Whitacre is a schoolteacher and enjoys teaching Pre-K students. She is also a grandmother and has one son.

ABOUT THE AUTHOR

Rev. Frances W. Cox is a retired educator of 33 years. She is an artist, an illustrator, and a writer of Christian books. Her parents were adamant about making certain she was religiously trained. She grew up in a home where she was in church at least three times a week. She met her late husband, Rev. Wendell M. Cox, in college. Three children were born to this union.

Rev. Cox attended Christian colleges where she received a Bachelor's degree in Science at Claflin University. She received graduate degrees in the Natural Sciences and Educational Leadership at Clemson University.

She received a Post Graduate Divinity degree in Christian Leadership at Liberty University's Theological Seminary. She pastored a church for fifteen years. She is the founder of two non-profit organizations.

Rev. Cox has developed a special connection with the spiritual realm since childhood and has carried this relationship throughout her adult life. She has spiritual dreams, visions, and holds daily conversations with the Holy Spirit.

www.ingramcontent.com/pod-product-compliance
Lightning Source LLC
Chambersburg PA
CBHW040408010526
44108CB00045B/2726